Scottish Mountaineering Club
Climbers' Guide Books

BEN NEVIS

J. R. Marshall

SCOTTISH MOUNTAINEERING TRUST

EDINBURGH

First published in Great Britain 1969 by
THE SCOTTISH MOUNTAINEERING TRUST

Copyright © 1969 by
The Scottish Mountaineering Trust

First edition 1954
Second edition 1962
First edition New Series 1969

Designed by West Col Productions

SBN 901516 07 4

WHOLESALE DISTRIBUTORS
West Col Productions
1 Meadow Close
Goring Reading RG8 OAP
Berkshire England

Set in Monotype Baskerville Series 169
Printed in England by
Bradley & Son Ltd, Reading

Scottish Mountaineering Club
Climbers' Guide Books

BEN NEVIS

General Editor: ARTHUR EWING

A

CONTENTS

ILLUSTRATIONS

Altitude and proximity to the western seaboard expose
Ben Nevis to weather conditions probably unique in Europe.
Summit readings taken during the 13 years occupation
of the Observatory show an average of 261 gales a year
with wind velocities exceeding 50 miles per hour, mean
monthly temperatures for the summer months barely above
those experienced during winter at the base of the mountain
and a clear summit for less than 30 per cent of the time.

Such conditions in conjunction with the Alpine scale of
the mountain, particularly under winter snows, should
ndicate the need to apply mountaineering caution to the
full when tackling any route on the Northern precipice
while on the other hand heightening your appreciation
when a fine day is encountered.

Investigating the mountain proved a great experience
and one which I hope users of this guide will share and so
help to extend a growing awareness of the magnificent
qualities of Ben Nevis.

Finally it should be noted that this edition of the guide
is founded on the invaluable work of preceding authors
to whom we all remain indebted.

J. R. MARSHALL
Edinburgh, *April* 1969

Ben Nevis, 4406 ft., is situated $4\frac{1}{4}$ miles East-south-east of Fort William. The mountain has three subsidiary tops:—

1. Càrn Dearg (pronounced Carn Jarrack) (3348 ft.) is the South-west spur of Ben Nevis and lies 1 mile South-west of the summit.
2. Càrn Dearg (3961 ft.) is the North-west spur of Ben Nevis and lies $\frac{3}{4}$ mile North-west of the summit.
3. Meall An t-Suidhe (pronounced approx. Melantee) (2322 ft.) which is 2 miles North-west by West of the summit.

The mountain takes the form of an elevated plateau occupied by Ben Nevis and the subsidiary summit of Càrn Dearg (3961 ft.). The two other tops, Càrn Dearg (3348 ft.) and Meall An t-Suidhe, bulwark the main mass. The Western and Southern aspects which overlook Glen Nevis are mainly steep grassy slopes containing some excellent gullies and short exposures of rock. By contrast the North-east face falls abruptly from the plateau to present a complex precipice of magnificent scale almost 2 miles in extent.

The ordinary route to the summit of Ben Nevis is by the pony track constructed in connection with the old Observatory. Leave Fort William by the North road, cross Nevis Bridge and then take the road on the right to reach Achintee Farm where the pony track starts. It climbs the steep slope of Meall An t-Suidhe to reach the col between that top and Càrn Dearg (3961 ft.). Then rising above the Lochan Meall An t-Suidhe at nearly 2000 ft. it turns back across the Red Burn to ascend a series of zigzags up the scree-covered slopes to reach the plateau near the top of Number Three Gully. A steep 'short cut' rises to the right before the Red

Burn. On the plateau the track passes near to the precipices. As some of the gullies extend far into the plateau it is necessary to keep a good look out in misty weather and particulary in winter when large cornices may project far over the precipice.

To gain the track from the Glen Nevis Youth Hostel, cross the River Nevis by foot bridge and ascend steeply up the slope of Meall An t-Suidhe to reach the pony track near the first zigzag.

To reach the Charles Inglis Clark Memorial Hut, quit the track above Lochan Meall An t-Suidhe and continue Northwards, keeping almost level to the far slopes of the Bealach. Here a path can be found which, after descending perhaps 100 ft., bears North-easterly to contour under the Northerly face of Càrn Dearg (3961 ft.). A large boulder, known as the Luncheon Stone, will be seen on the left of the track. The Hut is located at a height of nearly 2200 ft. close to the Allt a' Mhuilinn, just above its junction with the burn from the Lochan na Ciste.

Though not a right of way, the old Banavie route can also be used as an approach to the Hut. Start from the distillery near Lochy Bridge and cross the main railway line, where a well defined track leads to a small gauge railway line. Follow this to the left for a few hundred yards, cross a small bridge, then turn up the slope diagonally on the right to reach the Allt a' Mhuilinn where the stream is dammed. Cross the stream and follow a track on its North-east bank to reach the Hut. Excellent views of the cliffs are obtained from this track.

The ascent to the Hut carrying a normal week-end pack requires about $2\frac{1}{2}$ hours by the route from Achintee and about 2 hours by the distillery track.

An alternative start to this route can be made about one mile East of the distillery. From this point a track leads under the main railway, then directly to cross the small gauge railway just left of the Allt a' Mhuilinn. The track then follows the left side of the river to join the other track at the small dam.

From Steall follow the Allt Coire Giubhsachan for a mile or more, then bear North-west to cross the Càrn Mor Dearg Arête and descend into Coire Leis to reach the foot of the cliffs or the C.I.C. Hut; or from the Arête bear Westwards to reach the summit of Ben Nevis.

TOPOGRAPHY AND NOMENCLATURE

The climber approaching Ben Nevis by the Allt a' Mhuilinn will pass Càrn Dearg N.W., on his right. The first large buttress is Castle Ridge which projects low down into the glen. Next is Càrn Dearg Buttress and between these lies Castle Corrie which contains the Castle itself rising from a higher level and is demarcated by North and South Castle Gullies. Raeburn's Buttress lies between the Castle and Cousin's Buttress which in turn is connected to Càrn Dearg Buttress by the North Wall of Càrn Dearg. Beyond the Càrn Dearg Buttress scree slopes lead up to Number Five Gully. Then comes the Trident with its three buttresses, and beyond it Number Four Gully, then Creag Coire na Ciste. Next is Number Three Gully which is the arbitrary dividing line between Càrn Dearg and Ben Nevis proper. Here the cliffs bend at a wide angle so that the precipice of Ben Nevis faces almost due North. Adjoining Number Three Gully is Number Three Gully buttress, then the Comb and numerous minor buttresses which lead round to the Tower Ridge. This is the first major buttress of Ben Nevis and it projects North-eastwards far into the glen to terminate in the Douglas Boulder. In the wide angle between Càrn Dearg and the Tower Ridge lies Coire na Ciste, with a tiny lochan nestling in the hollow.

East of the Tower Ridge, the great Observatory Gully (Number One Gully) branches in its upper third to form Tower Gully on the West and Gardyloo Gully on the East with Gardyloo Buttress between. Farther still to the East lie Observatory Buttress then Point Five Gully, Observatory Ridge followed by Zero Gully which divides the ridge from the great mass of the North-east Buttress. This projects far into the glen to terminate in a rocky platform not unlike the Douglas Boulder in formation. Beyond this is Coire Leis which is bounded by the crescentic Càrn Mor Dearg Arête on the South-east.

The summit plateau presents a large area with only comparatively gentle slopes. A good idea of the configuration of the mountain can be gained by following the edge of the plateau. From the top of Castle Ridge to the summit of Càrn Dearg N.W. (3961 ft.) is about a quarter of a mile. It is nearly half a mile from the Cairn to the top of Number Three Gully sloping gently down, then up and down. Thereafter about half a mile and a rise of 500 ft. lead to the top of Ben Nevis (4406 ft.). The Observatory is a few feet from the cairn, just behind the top of Observatory Buttress. The former stands about midway between the tops of the Tower Ridge and the North-east Buttress, which are respectively 250 and 300 yards distant. The Arête leading to Càrn Mor Dearg leaves Ben Nevis about 300 yards beyond the top of North-east Buttress. To find the Arête in mist, steer 130° (true) from the Observatory for 400 yards, descending somewhat, then turn due East. In view of numerous tragedies that have occurred on this route, marker poles have been erected to safeguard parties making the descent. The bearing from the summit must be maintained and on no account should any deviation to the left be allowed or risked. The Arête gradually curves round to the left until its direction is true North leading to the summit of Càrn Mor Dearg (4012 ft.). Magnificent views of the Ben Nevis cliffs may be obtained from this top and from the continuation of the Ridge to Càrn Beag Dearg. On the South-east side of the Càrn Mor Dearg Arête, Coire Giubhsachan leads down to Steall in Upper Glen Nevis.

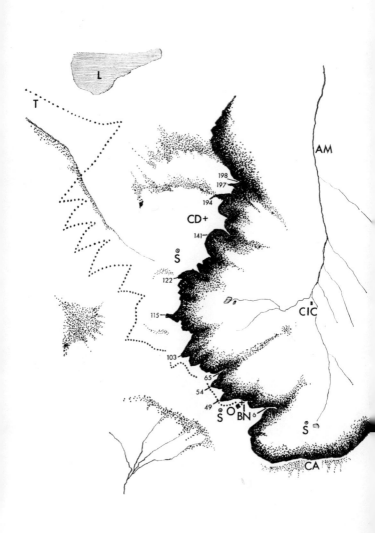

BN	Ben Nevis Summit, 4406 ft.
CD	Càrn Dearg Summit, 3961 ft.
CA	Càrn Mor Dearg Arête
L	Lochan Meall An t-Suidhe
AM	Allt na Mhuilinn
T	Pony Track from Achintee
O	Observatory Ruin
CIC	Charles Inglis Clark Hut (S.M.C.)
S	Refuge Shelters

Route No.

6	North-east Buttress, Ordinary Route
49	Gardyloo Gully
54	Tower Gully
65	Tower Ridge Original Route
103	Number Two Gully
115	Number Three Gully
122	Number Four Gully
141	Number Five Gully
194	South Castle Gully
197	North Castle Gully
198	The Castle Ridge

NOTES ON THE USE OF THIS GUIDE

(a) *For Rock Climbs the following terms have been used:*—
Easy
Moderate
Difficult
Very Difficult
Severe
Very Severe
The above gradings relate to rubber soles and dry conditions.
(b) *Winter Routes:*—
Classification of routes under snow and ice is at best a haphazard affair. Considerable variation can occur throughout a season, dependent on the qualitative or quantitative condition of snow and ice present on the mountain.

Despite these variations, it is considered worthwhile to adopt the separate grading system for winter routes, as presented in other guides of this series.

The grading is based on observation and knowledge of conditions over a period of years and should provide a reasonable indication of the difficulties to be met.

It must however be stressed that grading is based on average conditions and climbers new to the mountain should carefully assess from the guide or local advisers any serious variation in prevailing conditions before attempting some of the more serious expeditions.

GRADE I
Uncomplicated, average angled snow climbs, having no pitches under adequate snow conditions.

These routes can on occasions present cornice difficulties, or have dangerous outruns in the event of a fall.

GRADE II

Gullies containing either individual or minor pitches; or high angle snow with difficult cornice exits. The easier buttresses which under winter cover provide more continuous difficulty. Probably equates to the technical standard of Very Difficult.

GRADE III

Serious climbs which should only be attempted by parties experienced in winter ascents. Probably equates to the technical standard of Severe.

GRADE IV

Routes which are either of sustained difficulty or climbs of the greatest difficulty yet too short to be included under Grade V.

GRADE V

Routes of sustained difficulty which provide serious expeditions only to be climbed when conditions are favourable.

NOTE: A route must be truly under snow and ice to be considered as a winter ascent.

LEFT AND RIGHT:—

The terms 'left' and 'right' refer only to a climber facing the mountain.

ROPE LENGTHS:—

A minimum length of 120 ft. is recommended for a rope of two climbers.

HEIGHTS:—

Heights of individual pitches are related to rope lengths and should be sufficiently correct. Overall heights of routes are based on the summation of pitch heights with minor allowances. Whilst not necessarily correct, these should be sufficient to indicate the scale of any route.

MAPS:—

Ben Nevis. Lat. 50° 48′; W. long. 5° 1′. Ordnance Survey Map, one inch to one mile scale, Sheet 47, new series (Popular Edition); Sheet 53, old series. Bartholomew's Revised Half-inch Map, Sheet 15, old series; Sheets 50 and 51, new series.

ACCOMMODATION:—

Accommodation is available in the S.Y.H.A. Hostel in Glen Nevis, Steall Cottage (J.M.C.S.) in Upper Glen Nevis or the C.I.C. Memorial Hut (S.M.C.) by the Allt a' Mhuilinn, under the North Face of the mountain.

Good hotel accommodation is also available in the Fort William area.

INDEX OF CLIMBS AND
RECOMMENDED ROUTES

The recommended routes have been chosen as, in the opinion of the author, they typify best the unique character of climbing on Ben Nevis. At the same time it is hoped that these recommendations will not inhibit the more adventurous climber. The recommended summer climbs are prefixed by 'S' and the winter ones by 'W'.

Route No.

	108	Pigott's Route
W	109	**Green Gully**

NUMBER THREE GULLY BUTTRESS

W, S	110	Original Route
	110a	Original Route Variation
S	111	Knuckleduster
	112	Thompson's Route
	113	Gargoyle Wall
	114	Winter Chimney
W, S	115	**Number Three Gully**

CREAG COIRE NA CISTE

	116	South Gully
	117	Central Gully
	117a	Central Gully Variation
S	118	Central Rib
	118a	Central Rib Variation
	119	Wendigo
	120	North Gully
	121	North Gully Left Fork
W	122	**Number Four Gully**
	123	Number Four Gully Buttress

SOUTH TRIDENT BUTTRESS

	124	1934 Route
	124a	1934 Route Variation
	125	1936 Route
S	126	1944 Route

Route No.

NORTH WALL OF CARN DEARG

	169	Macphee's Climb
	170	Zag-Zig
	171	Easy Way
	172	Broad Terrace
	173	Flake Chimney
	174	Direct Start to Route B
S	175	Route B
S	176	Route A
	177	Caterpillar Crawl
	178	Flake Terrace
W	179	Harrison's Climb
	179a	Harrison's Climb Variation
	180	Harrison's Climb Dungeon Variation

COUSIN'S BUTTRESS

	181	Direct Route
	182	Ordinary Route

CARN DEARG SUMMIT BUTTRESS

	183	Colando
	184	Arch Buttress
	185	Arch Gully
	186	Surprise Buttress
	187	Surprise Gully
	188	Baird's Buttress

RAEBURN'S BUTTRESS

W, S	189	Raeburn's Route
	189a	Raeburn's Route Variation
	190	Continuation Wall
S	191	The Crack
S	192	Compression Crack

POLDUBH CRAGS

Route No.

HANGOVER BUTTRESS

209	Route I
210	Route II
211	Route III

CAVALRY CRACK BUTTRESS

212	Cavalry Crack
213	Storm
214	Heat Wave
215	Vampire
216	Fang
217	G-String

SECRETARY'S CRACK BUTTRESS

218	Secretary's Crack
219	Direct Route
220	Last Word

PINNACLE RIDGE

221	Original Route
222	Mechanic's Institute
223	Burma Road

REPTON BUTTRESS

224	Repton

PANDORA'S BUTTRESS

225	Phantom Slab
226	Dental Groove
227	Pandora
228	Flying Dutchman
229	Degradation

North-East Buttress

The North-east Buttress is the first of the great buttresses of Ben Nevis. Projecting East-north-east from near the summit cairn the buttress divides Coire Leis from Observatory Gully.

Coire Leis is situated at the head of the Allt a'Mhuilinn, under the crescentic Càrn Mor Dearg Arête which is the name given to the well-defined ridge extending from Càrn Mor Dearg (4021 ft.) to Ben Nevis.

Access from the coire is usually by the South-west slopes over scree or a uniform snow slope to gain the rim where it merges with the South-eastern slopes of Ben Nevis. These lower slopes can be very icy and a series of abseil posts have been erected to facilitate the descent into Coire Leis when such conditions prevail. These lie further to the right on steeper slopes, are of debatable value and possibly only to be used in emergency situations. Beyond these posts the rocks steepen, eventually to merge with the South-east flank of North-east Buttress.

A small shelter for emergency use is located on the bed of the coire, Grid Reference 173714.

The lower rocks of North-east Buttress form a minor buttress topped by the 'first platform', a large grassy easement. Thereafter the crest of the buttress rises in a great sweep to the plateau. The rocks on the left or East of the buttress are somewhat broken and eventually merge with the screes of Coire Leis. Routes recorded here are principally winter ascents.

The right flank of the buttress is formed by great slabs comprising the Minus and Orion Faces terminated on their right by Zero Gully. This is one of the great climbing areas of Ben Nevis.

The following routes lie on the East or left flank of the buttress, overlooking Coire Leis.

1 **Bob-Run**   400 ft.   III

I. Clough, H. Fisher, B. Small, D. Pipes, J. Porter and F. Jones, 10 February, 1959.

This follows the gully which separates the South-east face from a small buttress on the left.

Climb easy angled ice, 100 ft., then snow to the bifurcation, 100 ft. Either fork can now be followed. Each contains a short ice pitch then snow to finish. *Diagram*, p. 40.

2 **Cresta Climb**   900 ft.   III

T. W. Patey, L. S. Lovat and A. G. Nicol,   16 February, 1957.

The route follows a hanging snow gully which in its lower reaches terminates at a rocky spur some 300 ft. above the screes. Start well to the right of this spur, climb a raking ice shelf, 250 ft., to gain a small gully which leads up the right side of the rocky spur to its top. Climb the snow gully above for 600 ft. to a large ice pitch, traverse right across steep rocks, 100 ft., then break through to easy ground above. Time taken on first ascent 3 hours. *Diagram*, p. 40.

2a **Variation**   300 ft.   II

I. Clough and J. M. Alexander,   27 January, 1959.

The foot of the main snow gully is gained from the left
by a traverse across a snow shelf, access to which is by a
corner leading to its left end. This variation is easier than
the 'raking ice shelf' used on the original ascent.

3 **Slalom**   900 ft.   III

*I. Clough and D. Pipes with R. Shaw, J. M. Alexander and A.
    Flegg,*   6 January, 1959.

Start from a snow bay right of Cresta and follow a shallow
gully on the left. The climb goes up towards the rocky spur
and makes occasional traverses to avoid rock walls. Below
the spur make a leftward traverse 100 ft. to gain an easy
snow slope which leads to the final rocks overlooking the
top of the Cresta gully. Climb these to easier ground leading
to the top in 150 ft. Time taken on first ascent 4 hours.
Diagram, p. 40.

4 **Frost Bite**   900 ft.   III

*I. Clough and D. Pipes with J. M. Alexander, P. A. Hannon and
    M. Bucke,*   April 1958.

Start from the same snow bay as Slalom which lies to the
left of the steep rocks of the Eastern Climb. Ascend a steep
snow and ice groove on the right to reach a large snowfield.
Climb this 400 ft. to beneath a rocky spur. Traverse up
rightwards to the crest of a ridge under the steepest part of
the spur. Descend on the other side to the bed of a gully,
which is then climbed for 100 ft. to the right. Follow the
shallow gully to the left, climb an ice pitch, 100 ft., then iced
slabs up to the right for 100 ft. to gain the crest of the North-
east Buttress 60 ft. beneath the Mantrap. Time taken on
first ascent 5½ hours. *Diagram*, p. 40.

5 **The Eastern Climb** 1000 ft. Severe

G. G. Macphee and G. C. Williams, 22 June, 1935.

At the start of the ordinary route of the North-east Buttress before it traverses the easy ledge to the first platform there is a large grass slope. Move up this to easy angled rocks above. Scramble over the easy rocks to a 40 ft. wall, 100 ft. Turn the wall on the right, moving back left to pass behind a large pinnacle, 70 ft. The traverse continues above the wall by an easy walk, first to the left, then right to the base of a steep buttress, 300 ft. An easy chimney on the left leads to the edge of the buttress. This is followed until the angle forces an escape to the right. Move up, then back left to climb a slab corner by a thin crack under the right wall to gain a large stance on the crest of the buttress. Climb the very steep rocks left of the crest to reach a level ledge about 2 ft. wide. The rocks above are slightly overhanging; traverse to the right round a corner, 20 ft., then climb up, then left to regain the crest at a large ledge encumbered with large blocks. Alternatively climb directly from the ledge. From the left end of the ledge, which terminates in an exposed drop, move round a corner into a chimney. Climb this and continue by very steep rock on good holds to easier ground. From this point the North-east Buttress route can be reached about 150 ft. to the right over easy rocks but the climb continues directly to the steep final buttress. Climb this by a chimney splitting the crest or by surmounting an undercut block on the right wall to reach the top of the North-east Buttress. *Diagram*, p. 40.

6 **North-east Buttress (Ordinary Route)** Difficult

J. E. and B. Hopkinson, 6 September, 1892.

Traverse below the rocks of the lower section of the buttress until a broad ledge can be followed rightwards across the face to the crest of the ridge above the first great step to the 'first platform'. Above this point follow the narrow ridge to a steepening, turn this by a shallow gully slanting up to the left, then trend rightwards by short chimneys and grooves to gain the 'second platform' which is a sloping shelf on the crest of the ridge. The ridge is narrower and well defined above but presents no real difficulties for several hundred feet until progress is barred by a smooth overhanging wall. Turn this on the right by a corner with large steps or directly, working left from the right hand corner by a ledge until a bulge can be climbed on good holds. A little higher is the renowned 'mantrap', a short step on the ridge but the most difficult pitch on the route. Climbed direct it is Very Difficult, alternatively an overhanging chimney about 15 feet to the left can be climbed. The holds are less sound, the exit awkward, and it is at least as hard as the direct ascent. Beyond the 'mantrap' is the '40 ft. corner' which is climbed directly or can be turned on the left, to enter a small gully leading to easier rocks above the corner which lead to the summit plateau without difficulty. *Diagram*, pp. 40, 88.

VARIATIONS

        200 ft.   Very Difficult

D. W. Robinson, J. G. Robinson, J. G. McLean and A. R. Lillie,
    26 September, 1930.

The first steep section on the ridge above the 'first platform' can be climbed direct.

        250 ft.   Very Difficult

G. C. Williams and J. L. Aikman,   14 July, 1929.

Above the 'first platform' traverse out onto the right wall of the buttress and climb by slabs and grooves to regain the crest of the ridge.

60 ft.   Difficult

W. Brown and W. Tough,   25 May, 1895.

To avoid the 'mantrap' descend onto the right wall of
the buttress, then cross slabs to gain a gully which leads up
to the foot of the '40 ft. corner'.

WINTER   III

Both the original line of ascent or that via Slingsby's
Chimney are over steep snow to the First Platform.

Thereafter by following the easier of the summer ascent
lines, the ridge provides interesting climbing by snow filled
grooves and short walls, without serious difficulty until the
'Mantrap'. This is normally extremely exposed and awkward, particularly to parties tired by hard conditions lower
on the ridge. Fortunately it is short and failing the straight
ascent, the pitch can be overcome by combined tactics.
Alternatively, the Tough-Brown variation to the right
can be taken. Above, the 40 ft. corner can be climbed or
avoided on the left by a small gully which eventually leads
to the summit snows.

Under normal conditions allow 3–7 hours for the ascent.

The following routes ascend the minor buttress leading
to the 'first platform'.

7 **Newbigging's 80 Minute Route**   600 ft.
                                           Very Difficult

W. C. Newbigging and a Swiss companion,   21 August, 1902.

Some 150 ft. down to the right of the start of the broad
easy ledge leading to the 'first platform' of the North-east
Buttress a series of raking grooves and ledges lead up rightwards beneath a very steep triangular shaped crag.

The rake is the line of ascent, and it is followed, two short,
awkward walls being encountered before it terminates

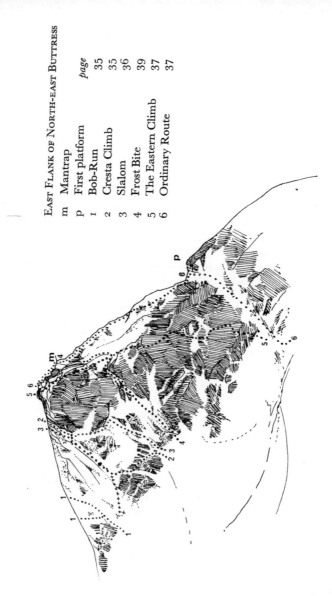

near the right hand arête of the buttress, 250 ft. Continue by the smooth left trending grooves above for 350 ft. to reach the 'first platform' of the North-east Buttress. *Diagram*, p. 88.

WINTER   III
J. R. Marshall and R. N. Campbell,   25 February, 1967.

The rake was climbed on mixed snow and ice with little difficulty to the first wall. This was climbed up to the left into a large groove below and parallel to the groove of the original line, 60 ft. The ascent of the groove on thin ice was delicate with few positive holds, 100 ft. A narrow 30 ft. chimney leads from the groove to easier mixed climbing above. Allow 3–4 hours.

7a Newbigging's 80 Minute Route (Right Hand Variation)   Severe
E. J. A. Leslie and P. D. Baird,   19 June, 1938.

Start about half way between the start of Newbigging's Original Route and the right-hand edge of the face (Raeburn's Arête) at a cairn about 120 ft. from the latter.

From a low rock ledge climb a groove to a large ledge at 20 feet, then follow a grassy rake up to the left for 100 ft. to belay. Break out right over a rib at the earliest opportunity and continue up to gain the left trending grooves under Raeburn's Arête, 100 ft., belay. Follow the grooves to gain the upper section of Newbigging's Route, 80 ft. Continue by these grooves to reach the 'first platform' after 300 ft. *Diagram*, p. 88.

7b Newbigging's 80 Minute Route (Far Right Variation)   275 ft.   Very Difficult
Miss N. Ridyard and Miss A. Smith with Miss N. Forsyth and Miss J. Smith,   7 July, 1938.

This route ascends the grooves parallel to Raeburn's

Arête. Start 30 ft. left of that route, climb the slab above
and move into the corner to a thread belay, 50 ft. Continue
up the slab; pass an overhang on the left by grooves and
ribs to belay at 80 ft. Follow the grooves to reach more
open climbing in two pitches of 150 ft. to gain the upper
section of Newbigging's 80 Minute Route. *Diagram*, p. 88.

VARIATION   Severe

G. H. Wiltshire, R. W. Cahn and L. Young, July 1945.

The overhang of pitch two was climbed and the corner
followed with minor deviations in two pitches of 60 and 80 ft.

8 Raeburn's Arête   750 ft.   Severe
H. Raeburn and Dr. and Mrs. Inglis Clark, 30 June, 1902.

The route follows the rock edge formed by the North and
East faces of the buttress.

Start at the lowest rocks directly under the arête. Climb
to a black overhang; turn it on the right to reach a grass
ledge and belay, 60 ft. Follow the arête above for 110 ft.
to belay. Traverse rightwards for 20 ft. then climb up to
regain the arête at the earliest opportunity, 130 ft. The
climb now follows the arête, with minor deviations, to the
'first platform', 450 ft. *Diagram*, p. 88.

8a Variation   150 ft.   Severe
A. T. Hargreaves, G. G. MacPhee and H. V. Hughes, 20 June,
1931.

After turning the initial overhang, ascend directly from
the ledge by slab grooves to join the original route in 150 ft.,
delicate.

8b Variation   180 ft.   Severe
S. Tewnion, J. Black and H. Convery, April 1949.

Start just right of the 1931 variation. Climb a crack to a

niche with a chockstone floor, surmount a 20 ft. slab (delicate) leading up leftward to a big ledge on the original route.

9   Green Hollow Route   680 ft.   Very Difficult

M. S. Cumming, E. J. A. Leslie and P. D. Baird,   6 April, 1933.

From the lowest point of the rocks work diagonally up rightwards by easy slabs to a grass ledge, 60 ft. Climb a crack on the right then traverse to a grass platform, 30 ft. Traverse up from the right end of the grass by slabs to gain a groove, 80 ft. This leads up to a small overhang. Climb up a crack to the left of the overhang; traverse right and belay on top of the overhang, 60 ft. Continue by the cracks above for two pitches of 80 ft. Climb up and right by a slab and groove; exit the groove on the left to gain a parallel groove, belay, 70 ft. Climb the groove to an overhang and exit right to gain the Green Hollow, 80 ft. Continue for 80 ft., leave the bay on the left to reach the arête, 60 ft. Continue up the crest to the 'first platform'. *Diagram*, p. 88.

WINTER   IV

J. R. Marshall and J. Moriarty,   February 1965.

On this ascent snow covered the lower rock, thereafter thin iced slabs and grooves were followed as for the summer route to reach the snow filled 'Green Hollow'. From the highest point of the snow, an iced slab led out left on to the final arête which is followed without difficulty to the First Platform.

The route provides a sustained ascent on ice, at least severe in standard, allow 4 to 5 hours.

10   Bayonet Route   600 ft.   Very Difficult

G. G. Macphee and A. G. Murray,   30 September, 1935.

The climb starts from the large grass platform which lies about midway between Raeburn's Arête and the foot of Slingsby's Chimney. Climb a rib of rough rock trending slightly left for 70 ft. to gain a grass niche. Traverse the rib on the left and continue up a grass groove to belay at 70 ft. Move left onto the rib and climb to below the left edge of the main overhang, 70 ft., belay. Gain the rib on the left and climb until a right traverse leads into a grassy bay, belay, 80 ft. Continue by the rib on the right of the bay for two rope lengths of 120 ft. and 70 ft. Climb a corner, exit on the left just above a prominent square cut overhang, 40 ft. Continue by easier rock for 80 ft. to gain the crest of the buttress. *Diagram*, p. 88.

10a **Variation**   110 ft.   Severe

J. R. Marshall and J. Stenhouse,   August 1959.

This provides a direct start by climbing the obvious corner from the left end of the grass platform. Two pitches of 70 and 40 ft. give access to the Bayonet Route below the overhang.

10b **Variation**   120 ft.   Severe

B. P. Kellett,   May 1943.

From the grass groove of the original route climb a slab for 30 ft. to a point below a V-notch in the main overhang; gain this by cracks, exit on the right, then, trending leftwards above the overhang, gain the original route in 90 ft.
N.B. The combination of these variations provides a good direct ascent of the face.

11 **Ruddy Rocks**   600 ft.   Very Difficult

G. G. Macphee and G. C. Williams,   15 June, 1935.

Start from the same ledge as Bayonet Route and a few feet to the right of that route. Above and on the left is a large overhang defined on its right by twin chimney cracks.

Climb directly to gain the cracks, 120 ft., belay. Continue, mainly by the left crack into grooves leading to easier climbing in two pitches, 150 ft. By the same line, climb to a small black overhang, 100 ft. Turn the overhang on the right by a chimney using mainly a smooth slab on the right wall, 60 ft. Easier climbing now leads to the 'first platform', 170 ft. *Diagram*, p. 88.

WINTER   IV

J. R. Marshall, R. Marshall and R. N. Campbell,   March 1967.

Approach by steep snow then climb the grooves which hold snow and ice well giving a sustained ascent over the first few hundred feet of the route.

Allow 3–4 hours for the ascent.

12   **Green and Napier's Route**   500 ft.   Difficult
E. W. Green and R. G. Napier,   8 June, 1895.

Start 100 ft. left of Slingsby's Chimney, a time hallowed misnomer given to the obvious gully leading up to the region of the 'first platform' of the N.E. Buttress.

Trending slightly rightwards climb difficult slabby rocks for 50 ft. to grass ledges. Continue more easily by a series of short walls and corners. Considerable variation is possible. *Diagram*, p. 88.

13   **Raeburn's 18 Minute Route**   450 ft.   Moderate
H. Raeburn and Dr. and Mrs. Inglis Clark,   23 June, 1901.

This route follows the series of short walls and corners which form the left or North Wall of Slingsby's Chimney.

Start 20 ft. left of the gully bed and climb by the line of least resistance. Considerable variation is possible. The route is generally used as a start to the main buttress climb, as it is one of the easiest approaches to the 'first platform' of the N.E. Buttress from the North-east.

The wall, under normal conditions becomes a steep unbroken snow slope.

The route may be used as a start to the North-east Buttress or, combined with a descent of the ledge of the original route from the 'first platform' it can provide an interesting expedition. It should be noted that the descent of the original route ledge from the 'first platform' can involve considerable step cutting on ice.

Allow $1\frac{1}{2}$ hours for the ascent.

14 **Slingsby's Chimney**   400 ft.   Moderate

G. Hastings, H. Priestman and W. Cecil Slingsby,   2 June, 1895.

The route follows the obvious gully which leads up the North-east Face to the region of the First Platform of the North-east Buttress.

Follow the bed of the gully on easy angled slabby rocks until a chockstone is reached at 250 ft. Hereafter the gully fans out. Trend leftwards to reach the 'first platform' in 150 ft. of climbing. There is a scarcity of belays throughout. *Diagrams.* pp. 56, 88.

14a **Variation**   150 ft.   Very Difficult

F. Greig, A. E. McKenzie and A. N. Other,   18 September, 1904.

From the chockstone climb slightly left of centre by mossy cracks on indefinite holds. A rather inadequate belay can be found about mid-height.

WINTER   I

First recorded ascent: *C. Donaldson and J. Russell*,   April
     1950.

A straightforward ascent on steep snow following the
normal summer line, allow 1 hour. The route provides a
good approach for the winter ascent of the North-east
Buttress.

Minus Three Buttress

THE MINUS FACE embraces the rocks bounded on the left by Slingsby's Chimney and on the right by Minus One Gully. The routes all lead to the crest of the North-east Buttress and are generally on clean slabby rock of sound quality.

The Minus terminology is extended in this guide to cover the rock contained by Slingsby's Chimney and Minus Three Gully on the right.

Minus Three Buttress comprises great slabs, chimneys and grooves leading up to the crest of the North-east Buttress.

15 **Right Hand Wall Route**   500 ft.   Difficult
N. W. Mowbray, D. Hotchkin and S. J. Jack,   16 September, 1929.

Follow the chimney line immediately right of Slingsby's Chimney to finish on rocks leading to the 'second platform' (belays as required). *Diagram*, p. 56.

15a **Variation**   300 ft.   Difficult
J. Jackson Murray, D. J. S. Harvey and W. L. Coats,   5 May, 1935.

This follows the slabby rock rib left of the 1929 Route. *Diagram*, p. 56.

15b **Wagroochimsla**   500 ft.   Very Severe
D. Haston and R. Campbell,   June 1964.

The route follows the crest of the broad rib between the 1929 Route and Platforms Rib.

Start midway between these routes and climb trending leftwards to turn the central bulge by an overhung corner. Continue rightwards by the crest to join the North-east Buttress at the 'second platform'. *Diagram*, p. 56.

16 **Platforms Rib**   420 ft.   Very Difficult

J. H. B. Bell, C. M. Allan and M. B. Stewart,   30 September, 1934.

Start at the foot of Minus Three Gully and climb by the bed of the gully for a short distance then move on to the rib on the left and follow this by a shallow groove to a belay at 75 ft. Continue by the rib to below a steep wall, 60 ft., belay. Climb the left edge of the wall to regain the grooves above and climb to a belay, 50 ft. Follow the line of grooves and chimneys above for 250 ft. to reach the crest of the North-east Buttress between the first and second platforms some 100 ft. above the former. *Diagram*, p. 56.

WINTER   IV

H. MacInness, I. Clough, T. Sullivan and M. White,   8 March, 1959.

The steep wall can provide serious difficulties on ice and on this ascent was surmounted using pegs. Thereafter the grooves above are followed with minor difficulties to the crest of the North-east Buttress. Allow 4–6 hours for the ascent.

MINUS THREE GULLY

This is the shallow gully which rakes up hard under the flank of Minus Two Buttress. The right wall of the gully is generally overhung, whereas it is possible to escape leftwards at several points from the gully on to Platforms Rib.

17   **Minus Three Gully**   520 ft.   Very Severe

J. R. Marshall and G. J. Ritchie,   July 1964.

Climb the bed of the gully to the foot of a steep groove pitch, 75 ft. Follow the groove for 20 ft., surmount a right-ward forking, slightly overhung crack, continue in the crack until the rib on the left can be gained, whence easier climbing leads into a large cave, 65 ft. From the back of the cave, traverse left then steeply up to follow the bed of the gully, 90 ft. Climb the cracks in the left wall to gain a rib which is followed to a short groove leading to a stance and belay in the bed of the gully, 90 ft. Continue by easier chimneys to the crest of the North-east Buttress, 200 ft. *Diagrams*, pp. 56, 88.

WINTER   IV

R. Smith and J. R. Marshall,   7 February, 1960.

Climb steep snow to the base of the gully, continue by mixed snow and ice to gain a deep cave at 100 ft. Exit by an ice wall on the left to gain a groove leading to the base of the next pitch, belay, 80 ft. Climb the groove above; finish by a short difficult wall at 80 ft. and continue on snow to belay at 130 ft. A further 50 ft. ice pitch leads to easier mixed climbing which gives access to the crest of the North-east Buttress.

The route is somewhat artificial as escapes can be made from below each pitch, leftwards onto Platforms Rib. Allow 5–6 hours.

Minus Two Buttress

Comprising great slabs, the buttress is readily identified by a prominent undercut nose above the lower third. From the lower rocks a raised crest edged by a great corner on the right leads to the nose, above which easier rock, climbable by a variety of lines, continue to an apparent tower on the North-east Buttress.

18 **Left Hand Route**   900 ft.   Very Severe

B. P. Kellett, R. L. Plackett and C. M. Plackett, 20 June, 1944.

Climb by the cracks which split the front of the prominent raised crest of the buttress to reach a ledge at the foot of a slab bounded on its right by an overhanging wall, 220 ft., belays. From the left end of the ledge descend the slab for 10 ft., traverse left round a rib to gain a slab which is climbed on small holds to reach a belay at 30 ft. This belay can be gained by a direct ascent of the slabs above the ledge. Climb the crack in the corner for 15 ft. then traverse left to the belay, alternatively make a diagonal leftwards ascent of the slab to the belay. Both these variations are more difficult and are more often wet. Continue up the left edge until it is possible to gain the rib on the right, belays, 120 ft. Easier climbing leads to the crest of the North-east Buttress at the level of the 'second platform'. *Diagram*, p. 56.

18a **Variation**   200 ft.   Very Severe

I. Clough, D. G. Roberts, G. Grandison and D. Miller, 1 June, 1963.

The variation ascends the groove immediately right of

Minus Three Gully to join the Left Hand Route at the foot,
of the 10 ft. descent.

Scramble up into the corner, this is normally wet so
move out left and climb a 'V' Groove; exit left to a stance.
Move up, then right into the main groove, to a thread belay
in the corner. Climb the slab, then work rightwards over the
overhang to join the original Left Hand Route. *Diagram*, p. 56.

19   **Central Route**   400 ft.   Very Severe

R. Smith and J. Hawkshaw,   May 1960.

Start a few feet to the right of the Left Hand Route on the
raised crest which is a prominent characteristic of the
Minus Two Buttress.

Climb by cracks to reach the nose of the raking belt of
overhangs above, 200 ft. Traverse right and climb the nose
by a thin crack to gain a slab; turn the overhangs above on
the left and continue to easier climbing, 130 ft. A choice of
routes leads to the crest of the North-east Buttress. *Diagram*,
p. 56.

20   **Right Hand Route**   900 ft.   Very Severe

B. P. Kellett,   20 June, 1944.

The route follows the line of cracks which lie a few feet
to the right of the well defined corner, which bounds Central
Route on its right.

Climb 30 ft. to a belay in the corner, continue delicately
by the slab or cracks above to a small stance and belay,
130 ft. Climb the steepening wall above for a few feet, then
traverse rightwards 15 ft.; surmount a bulge and traverse
left to a groove which is climbed to a belay, 130 ft. A further
60 ft. leads to easier ground above which the buttress,
though fairly steep, is climbable almost anywhere. *Diagram*,
p. 56.

21 **Subtraction**   900 ft.   Very Severe

J. McLean and W. Smith,   August 1959.

Start 40 ft. right of the Right Hand Route.

Climb the well defined groove for 110 ft. then take a peg belay below the left trending overhanging continuation of the groove. From the rib on the right surmount the overhang above and climb to a belay, 80 ft. Climb by the arête to a belay under a corner, 130 ft. Continue by the corner to gain Minus Two Gully at a peg belay, 140 ft. Cross the gully and climb up rightwards on Minus One Buttress to gain the second obvious groove; climb this to reach a belay on a grass ledge on the right wall, 100 ft. Climb the overhanging groove and continue to a belay, 140 ft. Easier climbing leads to the crest of the North-east Buttress. *Diagram,* p. 56.

22 **Minus Two Gully**   900 ft.   Severe

W. Peascod and B. L. Dodson,   29 August, 1950.

After 100 ft. of easy climbing the gully steepens and three chimney pitches of 80, 35 and 30 ft. lead to the foot of a well defined groove, topped by a triangular, black overhang. Climb to the overhang, then using holds above, traverse left to a stance and belay, 80 ft. (This pitch is often greasy).

Less difficult climbing leads in 200 ft. to a series of steep, greasy chimneys. Climb these, turning the overhang in the second chimney by the left wall and climb to a large block belay on the left, 90 ft. Continue by the crack above to reach the easy bed of the gully in 70 ft. A short distance above, the gully forks and the right branch is followed for 200 ft. to easier climbing giving access to the crest of the North-east Buttress. *Diagrams,* pp. 56, 88.

WINTER   V

J. R. Marshall, J. Stenhouse and D. Haston, 11 February, 1959.

On this ascent steep snow led to a bulging ice pitch some 30 ft. high; this was followed by sustained mixed climbing with the groove and overhang providing the greatest difficulties. The chimney above the overhang was entered to take an axe belay, thereafter a delicate slab traverse was made to the left to gain the upper chimney line which was followed with less difficulty to the steeper chimneys above. These were heavily iced but were climbed as for the summer route, which appeared to be the natural line of weakness. The snow filled bed of the gully was then followed to the bifurcation, whence the left branch was taken over ice filled easy angled chimneys to the crest of the buttress.

Allow 6–8 hours for the ascent.

Minus One Buttress

The buttress is narrow and defined by Minus One and Two Gullies. Steep columnar rocks lead to an easier middle section, thereafter an impressive crest seamed by great grooves imparts an impregnable quality to the buttress.

23   **North Eastern Grooves**   965 ft.   Very Severe

R. O. Downes, M. J. O'Hara and E. D. G. Langmuir,   June
1955.

Start at the middle of the lowest rocks of Minus One Buttress, 75 ft. Up to the corner, and exit right on to a glacis, 85 ft. Ascend a shallow groove in the wall above to a detached block at 20 ft. Climb it by the crack on its right, then climb short walls, moving left to a niche, 65 ft. Step right and climb easily to the top of a vast plinth. Step left into a wet groove and climb this for 75 ft. To turn the overhang, traverse left (above the stance) under a steep nose until one can climb this. Arrive on large ledges level with the overhangs on the right. Descend into Minus Two Gully and climb easy rocks on its far side. Emerge on to a glacis where the gully lies back, cairn. Traverse an obvious line to the right, back on to Minus One Buttress. Climb up to a stook of perched bollards; step past them gingerly and climb the chimney groove on the right (continuation of lower line) for 30 ft. Move right, along a ledge on to the open crest of the Buttress above the overhangs, running belay; bridge strenuously up a groove to a spacious terrace. Climb to the top of a 40 ft. pinnacle and go up easily for another 100 ft. to a leaning pedestal. The knife-edge arête beyond makes a delightful

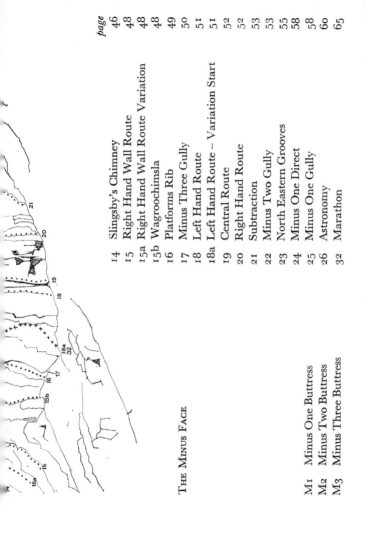

finish, joining North-east Buttress above the 'second platform'. *Diagram*, p. 56.

24 **Minus One Direct**   850 ft.   Very Severe

R. O. Downes, M. J. O'Hara and M. Prestige,   11 June, 1956.

Start as for North Eastern Grooves, 75 ft. Up to the corner, and exit right onto a glacis, 85 ft. Ascend a shallow groove in the wall to a detached block at 20 ft. Climb it by the crack on its right, then climb short walls, moving left to a niche, 65 ft. Step right and climb easily to the top of a vast plinth, 80 ft. Traverse right on to a nose above the overhang and ascend to a ledge. At the right hand end of the ledge is an undercut groove; pull into this and climb it until it is possible to follow a ramp up to the right, finishing at a block on a platform. A peg was used, 100 ft. Move up to the crack. Climb an overhang into it and continue up the wide crack above to the Meadow. Stance at the great detached flake well seen from Observatory Ridge, 85 ft. Climb grooves on the left-hand side of the gully to a small stance, 60 ft. Continue up the corner until one can traverse left across a loose wall into a fine niche, 70 ft. Step left on to the crest of the buttress and climb cracks and slabs above to the great terrace, 140 ft. Climb to the top of the 40 ft. flake, then up the crest easily to a curiously poised pedestal, 90 ft. Follow the narrow shattered arête beyond to join the North-east Buttress above the 'second platform'. *Diagram*, p. 56.

25 **Minus One Gully**   800 ft.   Very Severe

I. S. Clough and D. Pipes,   5 July, 1958.

Enter the gully to climb easy rock and one pitch of 50 ft., to gain a point under the first overhang. Start by bridging, gain the left wall and climb until a short traverse leads to a stance on the edge of Minus One Buttress, 70 ft. Climb the edge to below the gully overhang, surmount this with the aid of a peg, finish by a slab to reach a stance, 20 ft. Move up the gully to the foot of the next pitch; climb this by bridging; quit the gully by a delicate right traverse on slabs to a detached flake, 70 ft. Climb the rib above on small holds to gain a grassy stance, 30 ft., peg belay. Continue by the corner above (2 pegs and 2 wedges used), 30 ft. Climb by cracks and chimneys for three pitches, 200 ft., to re-enter the gully which is followed easily to an amphitheatre. Move up left on to the final arête of Minus One Buttress and follow this to the crest of North-east Buttress, 400 ft. *Diagrams*, pp. 56, 88.

Orion Face

This wedge shaped face fans from Minus One Gully on the left, to Zero Gully on the right. The middle of the face contains a shallow depression which holds snow into the late spring. Easily identifiable this is known as the 'basin'. It is a place of intersection for most routes on the face. The name Orion was given from a fancied resemblance of the principal routes on the face to the configuration of the stars in the constellation Orion, with the 'basin' corresponding to the belt of Orion.

26 **Astronomy**   955 ft.   Very Severe

I. S. Clough and G. Grandison,   13 June, 1962.

Start from a grassy ledge about 50 ft. right of the foot of Minus One Gully to follow a line of cracks and grooves parallel to and right of Minus One Gully.

Move diagonally right to a slabby crest and follow grassy grooves to flake belays, 120 ft. Up, then right, to a large spike belay below twin grooves, 65 ft. Climb the right hand groove, then trend right to the corner bounding the Great Slab Rib on its left; climb this to a spike belay, 120 ft. Continue up the corner, then traverse left to a chockstone belay above a smooth groove (junction with Minus One Gully's 'avoiding' pitches), 80 ft. Climb cracks to belay at the foot of a big slab corner, 60 ft. Continue by a crack in the slab to a stance and chockstone belay, 50 ft. Climb the flake chimney and corner above to belay, 70 ft. Move up 15 ft., traverse right and climb a groove to a stance under an overhang, peg belay, 70 ft. Turn the overhang on the

right to follow a crack to an overhung corner, 35 ft. Traverse
right 20 ft. then trend back left to regain the crack line, 85 ft.,
peg belay. Break out left and continue more easily to grassy
ledges and a chockstone belay, 130 ft. Traverse left up to a
grassy corner and continue left to the crest of the North-east
Buttress, 70 ft. *Diagram*, p. 56.

27 **The Long Climb**   1400 ft.   Severe

J. H. B. Bell and J. D. B. Wilson, June 1940.

Climb an easy angled, ochre coloured rib on the left of
Zero Gully to reach a small platform, 200 ft. From the left
of the platform a rib leads up steeply to the base of the 'great
slab rib', a prominent feature of the route. Round the rib
on the left then move up to gain the foot of the 'great slab
rib', 150 ft. Alternatively, climb the rib direct or climb by a
groove on the right side of the rib. These variants are considerably harder than the original route, with difficulties
contained mainly in the lower rocks. Traverse right onto
the crest of the 'great slab rib' and climb by parallel cracks
to reach a recess and belays, 100 ft. Move out and up to
the right and climb more easily to reach 'the basin',
150 ft. Cross the 'basin' and climb to the foot of the 'second
slab rib', 120 ft. Climb the rib by the slab edge, high up
a steepening is turned by the left wall (or climbed direct,
very severe) to regain the crest, 100 ft., belay. The wall
above is awkward and should be turned on the left or right
to reach a stance and belay, 30 ft. The climb is now on easier
rocks and many variations are possible. The original route
trends up to the left aiming for the base of yet another great
slab, some 200 ft. high. This is not climbed but the rocks
on its right are taken to a niche near the top, whence a
short difficult pitch leads to the top of the slab. Easier

climbing then leads to the crest of the North-east Buttress. *Diagram*, p. 88.

27a   Variation—Alpha   500 ft.   Severe

J. H. B. Bell and G. Dwyer,   August 1940.

Above the 'great slab rib', continue directly by a slab rib, then rightwards to the crest of the left edge of the 'basin', just below an overhanging section, 150 ft.

Climb a raking groove, then make an awkward exit to stance and belays above, 80 ft. Continue more easily to the crest of the North-east Buttress. *Diagram*, p. 88.

27b   Variation—Zeta   350 ft.   Very Difficult

J. H. B. Bell and V. P. Roy,   July 1935.

Climb the left rim of the 'basin' to the overhang; traverse right then obliquely up left to easier ground. Continue by easier rocks leftwards to the crest of the North-east Buttress. *Diagram*, p. 88.

WINTER   V

R. Smith and R. K. Holt,   January 1959.

A good plating of snow and ice was present on this ascent. The approach slabs were climbed on snow and ice to the 'great slab rib'. This was turned by the left and presented great difficulties, thereafter more easily to the 'basin'. Epsilon Chimney was then followed to the crest of the North-east Buttress. Time taken on this ascent, 12 hours.

27c   V–Traverse   300 ft.   Difficult

J. H. B. Bell and G. Dwyer,   August 1943.

This route can be used as access to or from the 'basin'.

Traverse the lower left rim of the 'basin' to follow slab rakes leading leftward towards a prominent V-notch on North-east Buttress.

VARIATION   450 ft.   Difficult

B. P. Kellett,   August 1943.

From the V-notch make a descending traverse to cross just above the 'basin'. Continue rightward under the second slab rib then by an ascending line, cross Zero Gully to Observatory Ridge.

28 **Epsilon Chimney**   350 ft.   Difficult

J. H. B. Bell and J. E. McEwan,   June 1940.

This is probably the easiest upper exit from the 'basin'. Climb a short, narrow chimney readily identified at the back of the 'basin', then by a left raking ascent climb to the crest of the North-east Buttress. *Diagram,* p. 88.

29 **Beta Route**   320 ft.   Very Severe

J. H. B. Bell and G. Dwyer,   August 1940.

The route is a direct ascent from the lower reaches of Slav Route to the 'basin'.

Climb to the top of the second steep pitch of Slav Route. Traverse to the left end of the large platform which is defined by the lower reaches of a deep chimney. Climb the rib to the right of the chimney to a stance, 100 ft. Move up rightwards over difficult smooth slabs to easier climbing and a belay at 40 ft. Turn the steeper rocks above on the right, then climb directly to the 'basin', 180 ft. *Diagram,* p. 88.

29a **Variation**   150 ft.   Very Severe

B. P. Kellett, 1943.

From the belay above the second pitch climb directly

by easy slabs to belay at 50 ft. Climb the steep mossy face
above to a ledge at 50 ft. Another pitch of 50 ft. on easier
slabs leads directly to the 'basin'.

30 **Direct Route**   1400 ft.   V
J. R. Marshall and R. Smith,   13 February, 1960.

Climb steep snow to the foot of the wall, then by an iced
slab gain the left end of the broad ledge of the Slav Route,
100 ft. Continue by the steep ice chimney directly above to
a peg belay beneath a rock roof, 130 ft. Traverse left then
up by ribs and grooves to reach the 'basin' in two rope lengths.
Mixed snow and ice lead to the foot of the 'second slab rib'
which is turned by an ice wall on the right. Above, leftward
trending snow and ice grooves lead to the snow slopes
under the final tower of the North-east Buttress. The tower
was climbed directly by steep iced chimneys which gives
access to the plateau at its junction with the North-east
Buttress. *Diagram*, p. 88.

31 **Slav Route**   1000 ft.   Severe
Edo Derzag, Marko Debelak, and E. A. M. Wedderburn,
16 September, 1934.

Higher up Zero Gully another rock rib rises from the bed
of the gully; scramble up the rib until the rock steepens.

Climb to a small stance at 50 ft. where there is occasionally a placed peg; move out right and up to belay at 110 ft.
Continue up to the right to the edge of a steep slab overlooking the gully, then up left to a platform, 45 ft. Follow the
scoop to the left of the rib to a shallow cave, 50 ft., then move
right to a platform. From the right end of this platform climb
directly to easier ground, 100 ft. Continue by the rocks close
to the left of Zero Gully, with occasional difficulties. Near

the plateau, the route bears left to finish by chimneys and corners. *Diagram*, p. 88.

WINTER   V

J. H. B. Bell and C. M. Allan,   5 April, 1936.

This ascent hardly qualifies for a winter ascent of the above route as the rocks were in part clear of snow but patently justifies recognition.

The party ascended the lower snows of Zero Gully, then evaded the crucial section by ascending the partially iced rocks of Slav Route to re-enter the gully which was then followed to the summit.

See S.M.C.J. Vol. XXI p. 200.

32 **Marathon**   2000 ft.   Very Severe

G. Farquhar and I. S. Clough,   22 September, 1966.

The climb follows a long rising traverse across the Minus Buttresses and the Orion Face. It gives fairly sustained and very interesting climbing and includes several hard pitches. Pegs were used for belays as required.

Start up Minus Two Buttress by the Left Hand Route Direct Start and traverse right (from the junction with the normal route) below the Central Route overhangs to the edge of the corner of Right Hand Route. A short abseil is followed by the Right Hand Route crux. From the belay above, traverse right to climb the upper grooves of Subtraction to a grassy ledge on the edge of Minus Two Gully. Cross the gully to a small platform, descend slightly and cross to the 'vast plinth' on North Eastern Grooves, 60 ft. The crux pitch of Minus One Direct leads up to the right to the edge of Minus One Gully, 80 ft. Climb up 10 ft., make a delicate right traverse to a stance and belay in a corner in Astronomy, 50 ft. A slightly descending traverse leads to the corner formed by the 'great slab rib' of Long Climb which is followed to a grass ledge, 60 ft. Continue as for Long Climb to the foot of the 'second slab rib'. Follow a line obliquely right across slabs and continue in the same general line finishing near the final part of Slav Route, by a chimney to the right of a prominent prow. *Diagrams*, pp. 56, 88

ZERO GULLY
The gully lies in the bay formed by the Orion Face and Observatory Ridge. Over its length it rarely achieves the normal character of a major gully and more generally adopts the form of a great open groove.

33 **Zero Gully**   1000 ft.   Severe

W. Smith, G. McIntosh and M. Noon,   27 August, 1955.

Regrettably the gully has not been climbed by the writer and little information is available from the party of the first ascent.

After climbing the lower 200 ft., the party then roped up. Thereafter 300 ft. and few belays led to the great pitch which involved a run out of 140 ft. Easier climbing by scree with occasional pitches to maintain interest gave access to the plateau. *Diagram*, p. 88.

WINTER   Grade V

H. McInnes, A. G. Nicol and T. W. Patey,   18 February, 1957.

The winter ascent is a serious expedition and should only be attempted by parties experienced in advanced snow and ice techniques. The lower section of the gully presents sustained high angle ice climbing with minimal natural protection and exposure to spindrift avalanche in wind.

Under normal conditions, details are as follows. Climb the central ice groove to a stance on the left, under some overhanging rocks, 100 ft. Continue, avoiding the bed of the gully, by a very steep ice chimney above, 60 ft. Traverse into the gully by iced rock, 40 ft., then continue more easily to a stance under the next steep section, 100 ft. Climb a short steep wall, then move right to a groove which is followed to stance and belay, 100 ft. Continue by the pitch above, 140 ft., then more easily by snow and occasional short pitches to the plateau, 600 ft.

Allow 5–12 hours for the ascent.

Observatory Ridge

OBSERVATORY RIDGE is the name originally given to the slender buttress on the right of Zero Gully. In this guide the reference has been enlarged to embrace the rocks extending rightwards to Point Five Gully.

34 **Original Route**   1200 ft.   Difficult

H. Raeburn,   22 June, 1901.

From the lowest rocks climb easily to the rightmost end of an obvious terrace at 200 ft. Continue by slabs and short walls a little left of the crest to steeper rocks which are turned on the right flank of the buttress then by cracks and grooves to the easier angled crest of the ridge. The ridge is now followed with occasional difficulties to the plateau. *Diagram,* p. 88.

34a **Variation (Direct Route)**   250 ft.   Very Difficult

G. C. Williams, J. L. Aikman and *A. R. Lillie,*   31 August, 1930.

This climbs the steep front of the buttress avoided by the normal route on the right.

WINTER   III

H. Raeburn, F. S. Goggs and W. A. Mounsey,   April 1920.

The summer route is followed throughout. Generally the greatest difficulties are to be met on the rocks just below the easement of the buttress, but the ascent is quite sustained over the lower half of the route. The difficulties of this ascent vary greatly depending upon conditions and can be time-consuming under powder snow.

Under firm snow conditions, the ascent should be severe, allow 3–4 hours.

35   **Left Hand Route**   250 ft.   Moderate
J. H. B. Bell

Start from the foot of Zero Gully and climb easy slabs to gain the left end of the grass terrace. *Diagram*, p. 88.

36   **West Face: Lower Route**   800 ft.   Very Difficult
B. P. Kellett,   8 July, 1944.

Start about 100 ft. left of Point Five Gully.

Climb 100 ft. to a pointed block then continue to enter grooves above, which are followed in two pitches 50 ft. and 80 ft. to reach the foot of a vertical wall barring access to the crest of the Observatory Ridge. Continue by slabs to the right to reach a broad mossy rake, 120 ft. Follow the rake to the foot of a deep waterworn chimney, 120 ft. Climb the chimney to reach the upper section of the buttress, 100 ft. A little to the right of this point a shallow gully is followed over difficult rocks for two pitches then easily to reach the summit plateau, 350 ft. *Diagram*, p. 88.

WINTER   IV

W. D. Brooker, J. R. Marshall and T. W. Patey,   1 February, 1959.

Climb mixed snow and ice, on to the pointed block then follow iced grooves a little to the left of the summer route, which is rejoined at a steep snow bay under the vertical wall. The slab traverses, if thinly iced can be awkward (a tension traverse was used to cross the second slab on the first ascent). The chimney above carries heavy ice and may require much cutting. To this point the difficulties are sustained and the route exposed. Above, a shallow scoop leads without difficulty to the plateau. Allow 4–6 hours for the ascent.

37 **West Face: Upper Route**   600 ft.   Severe

J. F. Hamilton and J. H. B. Bell,   11 July, 1937.

This route follows the left edge of the great slabs which lie to the left of Point Five Gully.

Start at the foot of Point Five Gully and climb by the rocks on its left to gain a large recess, 100 ft. From the left edge climb to an overhang at 15 ft., traverse left then up to cracked blocks, 50 ft. Continue for a few feet in the groove, gain the rib on the left and climb to a block belay, 100 ft. Follow a groove on the right to its termination; traverse left then up to a ledge and belay, 90 ft. Traverse a rib on the right to enter a mossy groove, which is followed to belays, 100 ft. (Alternatively, climb the groove trending right to an obvious block belay then climb up and right around a rib to belays). Both of these pitches are exposed traverses above the slabs of the lower reaches. Continue up the corner by cracks to a belay, 60 ft. Round a rib to gain a sloping slab under a steep corner; climb on to an obvious block on the right wall then traverse left into the corner and up to belay, 80 ft. Climb the chimney above, turn the overhang by slabs on the right to gain the Girdle Traverse ledge. *Diagram*, p. 88.

38 **Pointless**   1000 ft.   Very Severe

R. Marshall and J. R. Marshall,   4 September, 1966.

This route follows a central line up the great slabs to the left of Point Five Gully.

Start a few feet left of the foot of the gully. Climb a groove leading to a large scree patch, 100 ft. (as for Upper Route). Continue by the crest of a broad rib, aiming for the foot of the obvious corner above to belay under slabs barring access to the corner, 60 ft. Climb the slabs slightly right of centre to a spike belay under the corner, 60 ft. Climb the corner, break out right (peg) and belay under another corner on the right, 90 ft. Follow the steepening corner to belays, 100 ft. Continue by the same line towards a narrow chimney and belays, 100 ft. Climb the chimney to join the ledge of the Girdle Traverse, 60 ft., cairn. Continue directly by slabs and grooves, 120 ft., thereafter, occasionally climbing, gain the plateau in 400 ft. *Diagram*, p. 88.

39 **Point Five Gully**   1100 ft.   Very Severe
M. Noon and G. McIntosh,   28 August, 1955.

This is the steep narrow gully which separates Observatory Ridge from Observatory Buttress.

From the foot of the gully climb slabs to a ledge and belay on the left, 110 ft. Continue up the gully until an awkward move must be made right into an overhanging groove. Climb this then traverse left and up to a ledge and peg belay, 120 ft. Climb direct to the overhang, move right on small holds onto a rib, climb this, then move left into the gully. Take a steep wall on the right to another rib and climb to a small spike belay, 120 ft. Follow the rib to a block belay on the right, 20 ft. Move left to climb by a chimney, 120 ft. Continue to a belay on the right, 20 ft. Climb directly by short overhanging walls, 120 ft. Follow the gully to a large ledge, belay on left, 120 ft. Continue directly to beneath a small scoop, no belay, 120 ft. Climb the scoop to a ledge, peg belay, 50 ft. Continue by the steep chimney above, 60 ft. Easier climbing now leads to the summit plateau. *Diagram*, p. 88.

WINTER   V

J. M. Alexander, I. S. Clough, D. Pipes and R. Shaw, 12–16
    January, 1959.

The ascent is a serious undertaking demanding adequate
skill and experience of Scottish snow and ice conditions.
Initially the gully was climbed by siege tactics, when succes-
sive sections were roped for the follow up parties, with the
full expedition occupying five days, or twenty-nine hours
of actual climbing. Subsequent parties have effected the
ascent in times ranging from 7 to 15 hours.

The lower reaches of the gully provide sustained high
angle ice climbing with minimal natural protection. Addi-
tionally this section is subject to minor avalanches which
descend with devastating effectiveness whenever wind
conditions are shifting powder snow from the higher crag.
In short, conditions of weather, snow, ice and party should
be well evaluated before attempting this expedition.

Under normal conditions the details are as follows.
Climb an iced slab to stance under wall, 100 ft. Move out
left on vertical ice then rightwards by an ice bulge to reach
a snow bay and stance, 30 ft. Climb ice choked chimneys to
a snow stance, 140 ft. Climb by a continuously steepening
ice wall, 50 ft., to reach the easier upper section of the gully.
Continue with occasional short ice pitches to the plateau,
500 ft.

Allow 7–15 hours for the ascent.

Observatory Buttress

About half way up Observatory Gully the buttress rises steeply from the screes on the left. It forms the broad mass of rock extending from Point Five Gully on the left to Gardyloo Gully on the right.

At mid-height the buttress is traversed by a great ledge broadening to the right and giving access to a junction with the foot of Gardyloo Gully and the exit from Observatory Gully.

40 **Left Edge Route**   400 ft.   Severe
C. M. Allan, J. H. B. Bell and E. A. M. Wedderburn, 13 September, 1936.

Start at the foot of the rib bounding Point Five Gully on its right. Climb the rib to belay, 100 ft. Continue by the steeper rocks above for 40 ft., then move right to belay. Climb the shallow groove on the left, then out right and up to gain the 'luncheon spot'. Gain the flake on the right, then move up into a groove and slab, 60 ft. Follow the grassy slab rake up to the right for 70 feet. Climb the steep waterworn groove above, moving right to finish at a ledge and block, 80 ft. Surmount the corner above, then another corner leading to the left to reach the easy terrace. *Diagram*, p. 88.

41 **Rubicon Wall**   400 ft.   Severe
A. T. Hargreaves, F. G. Heap and Ruth E. Heap,   13 September, 1933.

Start about 50 ft. from the left edge of the buttress and climb easy yellow slabs to a large ledge, 30 ft.

From the left end of the ledge, climb a rock rib to a ledge and block belay, 60 ft. Move right, climb into a groove which leads to a large ledge and belay, 40 ft. Traverse almost horizontally some 40 ft. right to an incipient gully, follow this then move out right to large block belay, 90 ft. Continue the traverse past a little buttress to a 'V' shaped corner; move out right then up to finish by a corner and rib, belay, 60 ft. Follow the corner or rib to a ledge and belay, 20 ft. From the right end of the ledge climb slightly left to a higher ledge, then by a thin crack and small groove to a stance and belay, 60 ft. The corner to the left is climbed to sloping ledges and an inconspicuous flake belay, 40 ft. Climb grooves, make an awkward right move onto a rib then up to a flat ledge. Surmount some blocks to gain a recess; move right (delicate) to reach a small ledge, belay low down, 80 ft. Then move up right into a corner with a large block in it; climb this to easier ground. *Diagram*, p. 88.

42 **Direct Route**   700 ft.   Very Difficult

A. T. Hargreaves, G. Graham Macphee and H. V. Hughes, 19 June, 1931.

Start 90 ft. to the right of the lowest rocks, in a shallow bay. Climb 150 ft. to reach stepped, awkward, short walls, which are climbed to a large platform. Traverse left, climb an awkward corner to a platform and belay. A series of walls and corners, leading up and slightly rightwards give access to a ledge with a large slab leaning against the left wall, thread belay. (As for ordinary route) Continue above, by steep slabs trending right to an overhang close to the chimney, turn the overhang on the left and climb to a recess, belay. Easier climbing leads to the middle terrace, 40 ft. Moving up to the left 200 ft. of scrambling leads to an obvious crack topped by an overhang. Climb the crack, turn the overhang on the right and climb to easier slabs. Gain the crest on the left by a chimney and climb to the plateau. *Diagram*, p. 88.

42a **Variation**   150 ft.   Very Difficult

W. M. MacKenzie, A. M. MacAlpine, W. H. Murray and J. K. W. Dunn,   30 August, 1936.

From the ledge with the large slab leaning against the left wall, finish by the slabs on the left.

WINTER   IV

D. D. Stewart and W. M. Foster,   23 March, 1952.

Ascend the buttress rightward by snow ledges and short walls to cross the icefall on the original route at about 350 ft. Finish by easier climbing on the upper section of the buttress.

43 **Ordinary Route**   650 ft.   Very Difficult

H. Raeburn,   28 June, 1902.

Start well to the right of the lowest rocks, directly below the obvious chimney splitting the buttress higher up and just to the right of a projecting rib of rock. Climb 30 ft. to a small shelf and belay. Traverse up to the right then back left to a large ledge, spike belay, 70 ft. Climb to a large block belay in a square corner, 60 ft. Move right a few feet then up left to a corner with a flake belay high up on the wall, 60 ft. Climb up close to the chimney to a thread belay behind a large fallen block, 50 ft. Climb the groove above, traverse right, then make an awkward step across the chimney to a large platform. Easier climbing leads to the broad ledge traversing the middle of the buttress. Finish by a square cut rocky buttress with giant steps to reach the summit plateau a few feet from the Observatory ruins, 300 ft. *Diagram*, p. 88.

WINTER   IV

J. R. Marshall and R. Smith,   February, 1960.

The lower rocks bank up well; steep snow with short ice steps are normally met on this section if the shallow depression in the centre of the buttress is followed.

The upper chimney crack is often ice choked and may present considerable difficulties. Above this section a broad ledge is gained which can be traversed rightwards to escape into Observatory Gully.

Continue diagonally leftwards to gain the crest of the buttress which is then followed with minor difficulties to the plateau.

The ascent should be at least severe, allow 4 to 5 hours.

44 **North-west Face**   250 ft.   Difficult

E. J. A. Leslie, W. H. Murray, E. A. M. Wedderburn and J. H. B. Bell, 12 June, 1938.

Half way up the right flank of the buttress is a large rock bay. Scramble from Observatory Gully to the back of the bay where there is a narrow chimney, this is the line of the route.

Start in a corner some 80 ft. to the right of the chimney and climb by steps trending left to stance and belay, 70 ft. Cross the slab on the left to belays, 20 ft. Gain the chimney and climb in two pitches to finish on the right, 160 ft., to gain a large ledge. From the ledge one can traverse right to gain an easy shelf and Observatory Gully, below the upper crags. Alternatively continue climbing up to the left to gain the crest of Observatory Buttress and the plateau, 350 ft. *Diagram*, p. 88.

Indicator Wall

This is the steep slabby face above and to the right of the great ledge which girdles the Observatory Buttress. Defined on the left by the small gully of the Good Friday Climb it extends rightwards to terminate at the deep, narrow Gardyloo Gully.

45   **Good Friday Climb**   500 ft.   III
G. Graham Macphee, R. W. Lovel, H. R. Shepherd and D. Edwards,   7 April, 1939.

From the foot of Gardyloo Gully traverse left along the easy terrace of Observatory Buttress to the foot of a narrow gully. Climb this on snow to a steep rock wall, 200 ft. Traverse right on ice for 35 ft. to a small gully. Climb up to the left on ice for 40 ft. and continue upwards more easily for 150 ft. to the foot of another small gully. Climb this for 50 ft., traverse right then up in 40 ft. to the plateau. *Diagram,* p. 88.

46   **Indicator Wall**   370 ft.   Very Difficult
J. F. Scott, J. T. Austin and W. Moore,   11 July, 1941.

From the easy terrace, start 150 ft. to the right of the gully used by the Good Friday Climb.

Climb by a groove to gain a recess and belay, 60 ft. Continue by the grooves on the left to reach a small terrace, belay, 60 ft. From this terrace traverse up left into the gully and follow the right wall to a large terrace in two pitches, 170 ft. Continue above, turn some cracked blocks on the left, then climb by grooves and slabs to the plateau, 80 ft. *Diagram,* p. 88.

46a **Variation**   150 ft.   Very Difficult

B. P. Kellett,   1 August, 1943.

Start 120 ft. up the original route from the small terrace.
Climb by the steep rib above to gain the upper terrace in
two pitches, 150 ft. This is no harder than the original
route but provides a more direct line of ascent.

47 **Psychedelic Wall**   600 ft.   Very Severe

R. Marshall and J. R. Jackson,   September 1967.

Start about 60 ft. left of Gardyloo Buttress, below a
large detached flake.

Climb up to gain the flake from the right, then up and
right to a ledge. Continue by the slabby arête on the left
(peg runner) to ledge and belay, 110 ft. Climb from the
left by an arête to gain the left edge of a mossy ledge, peg
belay, 100 ft. Ascend the corner above for 10 ft., traverse
left 10 ft. then by a 20 ft. wall, reach a ledge. Continue by
the corner crack above to belay on top of an enormous
block, 70 ft. Climb grooves and cracks rightwards to a
ledge beneath a prominent corner, 80 ft. By the deep crack
above, climb 20 ft. to beneath a large block, move out right
to climb by the right edge of a loose chimney to belay, 90 ft.
Gain good slabs, then finish by one of three corners in the
final wall. Scrambling leads to the plateau, 150 ft. *Diagram,*
p. 88.

48 **Observatory Gully**   1000 ft.   Easy

This gully, more in the nature of a small corrie, separates
the North-east Buttress, Observatory Ridge and Observatory
Buttress from the mass of the Tower Ridge.

Starting as an easy scree slope the gully gradually narrows
and steepens to terminate beneath a high rock outcrop.
On the left the lower reaches of Gardyloo Gully breach this

barrier and the rocks on its right are climbed to reach a broad terrace above. This terrace, continued left becomes the easy terrace of Observatory Buttress and, to the right, leads below Gardyloo Buttress, Tower Gully and extends to join the Eastern Traverse of the Tower Ridge. In direct continuation above is Gardyloo Gully.

WINTER   I

An uncomplicated snow ascent. Allow 1 hour for the ascent.

49 **Gardyloo Gully**   500 ft.   Severe

G. Graham Macphee and R. C. Frost, 5 August, 1935.

The gully is well defined; a number of short pitches lead to an awkward chockstone pitch, which is climbed by bridging. Easier climbing then leads under the great jammed boulder arch of the gully to the steep final chimney. Climb the first 30 ft. by bridging, to a stance and belay (better used as a runner). Continue by the chimney facing Gardyloo Buttress to good runners below the final cap stone, 20 ft. A further 10 ft. of chimney work with good holds under the roof leads awkwardly to the screes, 40 ft. below the summit plateau.

The second man should take precautions against falling stones, as there is a fair accumulation of debris on this final section. *Diagrams,* pp. 84, 88.

WINTER   II

G. Hastings and W. P. Haskett-Smith, 26 April, 1897.

The difficulty of the climb depends on the amount and condition of the snow. Normally a uniform snow slope leads to a through route by a tunnel of varying dimensions beyond which is a steep funnel. This is climbed by a short ice pitch of 20 to 30 ft. followed by a steep snow slope which leads to the cornice, which is sometimes very difficult and frequently double.

If there is a great deal of snow the through route and chockstone may be completely covered, and the climb will then be by a steep uniform snow slope. Allow 3 hours under normal conditions.

Gardyloo Buttress

The buttress consists of two ridges, of which the left hand is fairly well defined, with a shallow depression between them. The upper part of this depression opens out into a wide funnel with what is almost a gully at the back; most of the water from this gully drains down two long, steep, smooth grooves slanting down from left to right. Between the lower part of these grooves and the left-hand ridge is a very steep face of over 100 ft., and above that three more grooves running parallel to the two long grooves, with slabs on their left, walls on their right. They end after about 100 ft. at the same level as the foot of the funnel. Below the steep face and stretching right across the foot of the buttress is a 150 ft. band of easy-angled rocks climbable almost anywhere.

50 **Left Edge Route**   500 ft.   Very Severe

J. R. Marshall, G. J. Ritchie and R. Marshall,   June 1962.

Start at the lowest left hand point of the buttress at the foot of the Gardyloo Gully. Climb the crest above by awkward tilting grooves to belay by an old peg, 110 ft. Gain the slab above, turn a rib on the right, then climb directly to belay beneath a crack and flake, 60 ft. Climb the crack, move up right past an old peg, mantelshelf a sloping ledge then round a rib on the right to enter a shallow groove. Climb this 10 ft., move right to gain the left edge of a slab, follow the edge to belays, 100 ft. Continue up the edge 10 ft., traverse horizontally right to a groove which is climbed a few feet until a crack leads back left onto the crest and belays,

100 ft. Follow the crest by steep walls and steps to the plateau, 100 ft. and 50 ft. *Diagram*, p. 84.

51 **Kellett's Route**   400 ft.   Very Severe

B. P. Kellett,   22 July, 1944.

Start about 80 ft. right of the lowest rock. Climb easily to the foot of a corner, belay, 80 ft. Climb the left wall by cracks to belay, 40 ft. Traverse right beneath an overhang, then climb a bulge to gain a recess. Climb the corner with difficulty to reach easier rocks under the three parallel grooves, belay, 140 ft. Climb into the right hand groove and follow this to a stance and belay beneath a right angled corner, 70 ft. Climb the corner, move left to climb an easier corner leading into the lower rocks of the upper gully, 40 ft. Follow this with little difficulty to finish, 80 ft. *Diagram*, p. 84.

51a **Variation**   200 ft.   Severe

D. Haston and J. Stenhouse,   14 September, 1958.

This quits the final gully bed at its lowest point, to follow the left hand ridge in two pitches of 120 ft. and 80 ft.

52 **Smith's Route**   400 ft.   V

R. Smith and J. R. Marshall,   8 February, 1960.

Start directly below the lower end of the slanting grooves. Climb a snow and ice groove 120 ft. to the foot of the main grooves, peg belay. Traverse up and left, across the lower groove to easier climbing, turn up to a steepening, break out and up right on very steep ice to gain the left edge of the upper slab groove, which is climbed to the foot of the upper funnel, 150 ft. (A peg runner may be obtained at mid-height on this section). Continue easily by the funnel to the plateau.

A good plating of snow ice is recommended for this ascent. Allow 6 to 12 hours under good conditions. *Diagram*, p. 84.

53 **Tower Face Crack**   100 ft.   Moderate

B. P. Kellett,   16 July, 1944.

About half-way up Tower Gully traverse easily leftwards to the foot of a conspicuous crack. Climb this. *Diagram*, p. 84.

54 **Tower Gully**   350 ft.   Easy

*G. Hastings, E. L. W. Haskett-Smith and W. P. Haskett-Smith,
    25 April, 1897.*

This gully defines the right or West flank of Gardyloo Buttress, starting from the easy scree slope above the rock barrier in Observatory Gully. The gully is an easy scramble. *Diagram*, p. 84.

WINTER   I

An uncomplicated snow slope with the occasional large cornice. Allow 1 hour for the ascent.

55 **Eastern Traverse from Tower Gully**   Easy, II

H. Raeburn, J. Rennie and J. H. Wigner,   January 1904.

The continuation of the broad terrace under Gardyloo and Tower Gullies leads almost horizontally to the Great Tower of Tower Ridge where by continuing at the same level the ordinary route can be gained by turning either to the right or left of the large poised boulder which forms the 'through route' of the Eastern Traverse (see Tower Ridge). The tower gap (East Gully) leads up from this shelf about half-way along it and presents no difficulty. Traversing the Eastern Traverse then ascending this Gully to the Tower Gap provides an easy means of gaining the

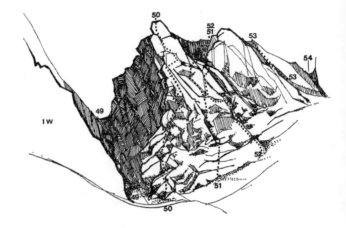

GARDYLOO BUTTRESS

Tower Gap and can be used as an escape from the Tower Ridge or as an easier access to the Tower Gap when the harder routes are impracticable. *Diagram*, p. 104.

In winter the traverse to Tower Gully should always be possible.

Tower Ridge

The following routes all ascend the Eastern or left flank of the Tower Ridge. For a general description of the ridge see p. 92.

56 **Tower Scoop**   200 ft.   III
I. S. Clough and G. Grandison,   4 January, 1961.

   Start under the rock barrier which terminates Observatory Gully at a point midway between the lower reaches of Gardyloo Gully and a deep cleft close in by the very steep flank of Tower Ridge. Climb a 70 ft. ice pitch to gain the scoop above; climb this finishing by an awkward corner and snow funnel to gain the terrace above directly below Tower Gully. *Diagram, p. 104.*

57 **Tower Cleft**   250 ft.   III
G. Pratt and J. Francis,   17 February, 1949.

   This route follows the deep cleft in the angle formed by the rock barrier terminating Observatory Gully and the very steep Eastern flank of the Tower Ridge.

   Enter the cleft and climb steep snow for 200 ft. Two openings lead through the roof above, climb the second tunnel by an ice pitch, very steep to start, to a snow saddle; mixed snow and ice then leads to the terrace. Allow 2–3 hours. *Diagram, p. 104.*

58 **Rolling Stones**   440 ft.   Very Severe
J. Cunningham and C. Higgins,   August 1965.

   Start 100 ft. to the right of the Tower Cleft.

Climb easily to rock shelves and belay, 80 ft. Traverse horizontally to the right by a good rock ledge beneath an overhanging wall. Climb a broken wall at the end of the traverse to reach a large ledge and belay, 40 ft. From the right end of the ledge, traverse 60 ft. to an overhanging recess about 4 ft. wide; climb this to gain a small ledge on the left, peg belay, 80 ft. Climb the corner above, traverse right to reach a wide crack, then climb to a good belay, 140 ft. Continue by easier rocks to reach the foot of the Great Tower, 100 ft. *Diagram*, p. 104.

59 **East Wall Route**   360 ft.   Difficult
C. W. Parry, G. Murray Lawson, M. Matheson and S. F. M. Cumming, 29 March, 1929.

Start a few feet to the right of the Tower Cleft Route. Climb by slabs trending rightwards to gain a grassy ledge beneath the steep upper wall, 200 ft. The ledge is followed without difficulty to near its rightmost termination where a short chimney gives access to rocks leading to the crest of the Tower Ridge.

The ledge can be followed further to the right where it leads on to the crest of the ridge. *Diagram*, p. 104.

WINTER   II
J. R. Marshall and R Marshall, February 1966.

The initial slab section presents mixed snow and ice climbing in two pitches to a ledge beneath a steep rock wall Steep snow is traversed rightwards to join the crest of the Tower Ridge. Allow $1\frac{1}{2}$ hours to the crest of the ridge.

60 **Echo Traverse**   Severe
L. S. Lovat, K. Bryan and N. Harthill, 15 July, 1956.

Climb the East Wall Route for 200 ft. then traverse right under the steep upper wall into the foot of a chimney recess.

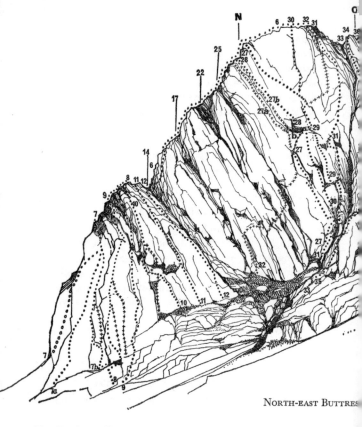

NORTH-EAST BUTTRESS

INDICATOR WALL

Climb the chimney, descend behind a block on the left, belay, 20 ft. This point may be gained directly from below. Gain a red slab to make a delicate traverse left, then climb to exit by a short chimney to belays, 30 ft. Continue by a left trending fault above, in two pitches, to reach the crest of the Tower Ridge at the Foot of the Great Tower. *Diagram*, p. 104.

WINTER   IV

J. R. Marshall and R. Marshall,   February 1966.

Mixed snow and ice led to the traverse ledge which was followed easily to the foot of the chimney. The groove to the left of the chimney was climbed to the belay. Great difficulty was experienced crossing the verglaced slab which was only effected by rope tension from a rock spike high on the left (this section should be considerably easier if thick ice is present). The difficulties continued above until a snow bay was reached. The fault above gave continuous cutting on ice covered rock in exposed situations.

A sustained route in the upper reaches, allow 3 to 4 hours to the crest of the ridge.

61 **The Brass Monkey**   420 ft.   Very Severe

J. R. Marshall and J. Stenhouse,   31 May, 1961.

This route follows the deep crack in the corner formed by the great projection of Echo Wall at a point about half-way up Observatory Gully.

Climb to the slab apex beneath the corner, 200 ft. Move up the corner about 10 ft., traverse rightwards using two pegs to gain the base of the crack, belay, 20 ft. Follow the crack in two pitches of 60 ft.; the last few feet were taken on the right wall to gain a ledge and belay. Re-enter the crack and climb to the crest of the Tower Ridge, 80 ft. *Diagram*, p. 104.

VARIATION

J. McLean and *W. Smith*,   1962.   15 ft.   Very Severe

The upper reaches of the crack were climbed directly to gain the foot of the final pitch and is the route since followed by most parties.

62 **The Great Chimney**   200 ft.   Severe

G. Graham Macphee and A. G. Murray,   28 September, 1935.

250 ft. to the North of Echo Wall a conspicuous, deeply cut chimney cleaves the flank of Tower Ridge. A large chockstone jammed far out is a useful identification characteristic. The rock scenery within the chimney is impressive.

Scramble to the foot of the chimney, 250 ft. Climb 20 ft. to a recess then 60 ft. to belays and a small chockstone. Loose rock leads in 20 ft. to the crux of the climb; a vertical block with cracks on each side. Climb the left crack on good holds within and, using sloping foot holds high on the left wall, gain easier climbing and a stance at 25 ft. From this point a restricted through route or an outside route can be followed to finish at a narrow saddle on the crest of the Tower Ridge below the Little Tower. *Diagram*, p. 104.

WINTER   IV

J. R. Marshall and R. Smith,   6 February, 1960.

A steep snow slope leads into the chimney which is climbed on ice to a belay under the crux, 90 ft. As in summer climb the left crack. Verglaced walls may make this section very difficult as on the first ascent when a sling was used on the holds inside the crack to provide a foothold. Mixed snow and ice leads to the crest of the ridge. This pitch is best continued to the crest of the ridge to obtain a good belay. Allow $2\frac{1}{2}$ to 5 hours for the ascent.

63   **Chimney Groove**   350 ft.   Difficult

First Ascent not recorded.

Climb vegetated rocks leading up right from the bay under the Great Chimney, 100 ft. Continue rightward to enter the groove, which is climbed to the crest of the Tower Ridge, belays as required, 150 ft. *Diagram*, p. 104.

64   **Lower East Wall Route**   400 ft.   Difficult

B. P. Kellett,   29 May, 1943.

Start about 200 ft. down the gully from the Great Chimney. Surmount a short overhang then follow easy ledges rightward to gain the crest of the Tower Ridge at the top of the first steep section above the Douglas Gap. *Diagram*, p. 104.

TOWER RIDGE, one of the best known names on the mountain, is the second of the great buttresses of Ben Nevis. Projecting far Northwards from the precipice, it separates Observatory Gully on the East, from the open, scenic, Coire na Ciste to the West.

A short distance above the C.I.C. Hut, the ridge rises from the glen at a level of 2300 ft., and sweeps some 700 ft. to the top of the Douglas Boulder, an imposing rock pinnacle separated from the main ridge by a deep cleft—the Douglas Gap. Above this gap the ridge narrows and after an almost level section, rises to the Little Tower. A short distance above this is the Great Tower rising precipitiously for nearly 100 ft. From the large cairn on the summit at over 4000 ft. altitude, a short descent leads to the Tower Gap, from which easy rocks lead to the summit plateau at a height of nearly 4400 ft.

There is one main route, with variations and numerous subsidiary routes which attain the crest of the ridge by the steep, varied East and West flanks.

On the first summer ascent the party ascended the ridge
to the foot of the Great Tower. Thereafter on the following
day accompanied by C. Hopkinson they descended the
whole ridge including the Great Tower by the Recess Route
and the Douglas Boulder by its North-east Face. They
were therefore the true pioneers of this great ridge.

On the first winter ascent the party went by the easy
rocks just above the foot of Observatory Gully to gain the
crest of the ridge a short distance above the Douglas Gap.
They turned the Great Tower on the right or Western
Side, apparently by the now designated Western Traverse.

65 **Tower Ridge**   2000 ft.   Difficult
J. Hopkinson, E. Hopkinson and B. Hopkinson,   3 September,
    1892.

It seems best to describe first the ordinary route established
through time and then variations. Strictly speaking the
Douglas Boulder should be included as the first part of the
climb.

If this is not done the ordinary route is to go round the
foot of the Douglas Boulder to the East side and climb the
rocks above the grassy bay to reach an ill-defined hollow,
from which the East Gully takes a definite form and leads
to the Douglas Gap.

It is easy to miss the lower section in mist but a useful
guide is the grassy bay.

From the Douglas Gap a few feet to the East of the highest
part of the Gap a moderate 60 ft. chimney gives access to
the crest of the ridge. The crest here is quite narrow and
almost level but soon steepens to a short pitch at an overhanging wall which is climbed up to and turned by a ledge
slanting to the right. Above this, moderate scrambling leads
by a series of rises to another almost level stretch. Two nicks

or depressions are crossed here, on the left of the second is the top of the Great Chimney. 150 ft. beyond this second cleft is the foot of the Little Tower. The route is by the rocks on the left edge then an awkward ledge rightwards can be followed to a corner. It is also possible to climb straight up the rock face.

At the top it is found that the Little Tower is in reality a step of the ridge.

Easy rocks now lead by the crest and should be followed to the very ramparts of the Great Tower under the North-eastern corner. To the East or left, a level grassy ledge, 2 or 3 ft. wide (The Eastern Traverse) is followed to cross an exposed but easy groove then round some rocks to enter the foot of a tunnel formed by a huge fallen block. From the top of this through route, a few feet more leads to steep but easy rocks on the right which are climbed straight up on good holds to the summit of the Great Tower, cairn. A slight descent is made to traverse a narrow crest leading to the Tower Gap. This presents little difficulty and the steep rocks on the far side of the Gap have good holds. Easier rocks beyond the Gap lead to a final steepening which is turned on the right by a ledge and groove to reach the summit plateau. *Diagram*, p. 104.

WINTER   III

J. N. Collie, G. A. Solly and J. Collier,   29 March, 1894.

In winter the Tower Ridge provides one of the finest mountaineering expeditions in these islands. Depending on the conditions, all degrees of difficulty may be encountered and the ridge has been known to baffle strong, experienced parties.

To anyone knowing the configuration of the ridge in summer, it should always be possible, given time, to force an ascent; but unless the ground is familiar it would be unwise to push the climb under bad conditions. Time being an important factor on a short winter's day, it is better to beat an orderly retreat than spend an involuntary night on the Tower Ridge. Allow $3\frac{1}{2}$ to 8 hours according to conditions and competence.

The Great Tower Variations

66 **Macphee's Route**   150 ft.   Very Difficult

G. Graham Macphee and G. R. Speaker,   1 September, 1935.

This route lies some 35 ft. along the Eastern Traverse
from the North-east arête below the second raking slab.

Climb 25 ft. to a block belay in the crack close to the
overhanging right wall. Climb to some large jammed
blocks and a flake belay, 25 ft. Traverse left to the outer
edge of the slab and climb 25 ft. to a large block belay under
an overhanging wall. Pull up on overhanging blocks then
continue on easy ground to the top of the Tower.

67 **Ogilvy's Route**   150 ft.   Very Difficult

H. I. Ogilvy and N. P. Piercey,   23 June, 1940.

This route lies some 20 ft. along the Eastern Traverse
from the North-east arête of the Tower, below the first of
the raking slabs.

Climb steep rocks to gain the foot of a corner, 20 ft.,
belay. Climb the steep slab corner leading up leftwards,
50 ft. Finish more easily to the top of the Tower.

68 **Pigott's Route**   150 ft.   Very Difficult

A. S. Pigott and J. Wilding,   23 September, 1921.

From the crest of the ridge, at the foot of the North-east
arête of the Tower, climb a slab on small holds to a ledge
at 15 ft. Traverse left round onto the Eastern wall, climb a
short chimney and exit by an overhanging block, 50 ft.
From a loose flake climb the slab to the left of the right

corner crack to the top, 30 ft. An easier alternative is to climb, from above the overhang, by a shallow chimney in a corner on the left.

69 **Bell's Route**   150ft.   Very Difficult

J. H. B. Bell and E. E. Roberts, 18 August, 1929.

Climb the initial slab of Pigott's Route then traverse up on good holds across the Northern face of the Tower making for the obvious block on the right. A difficult stride has to be made before the crack and the top of the block can be gained, 60 ft. Climb the steep scoop on good holds to the top of the Tower, 40 ft.

70 **Recess Route**   150 ft.   Difficult

W. W. Naismith and G. Thomson, 27 September, 1894.

From the foot of the North-west arête climb up to a broad platform, 15 ft. A chimney recess is visible 20 ft. above; climb from a large block into the recess, a thread belay is available on the right. Continue above the belay, on good holds to the top of the Tower, 60 ft.

71 **Cracked Slabs Route**   150 ft.   Very Difficult

J. W. Macgregor, April 1896.

This route lies a few feet to the right of the Recess Route. Start from the broad platform and climb by steep slabs provided with small cracks, 60 ft. Easier climbing in a shallow gully leads to the top of the Tower.

72 **The Western Traverse**   230 ft.   Difficult

J. N. Collie, G. A. Solly and J. Collier, 29 March, 1894.

Start under the North-west arête, i.e. the right-hand edge of the Tower. Make a level traverse rightwards negotiating an awkward corner to reach an obvious ledge. This point can be gained more easily by a lower traverse line. Follow the ledge to a chimney with a projecting far wall; cross the chimney with difficulty and exposure to reach another ledge. Follow this up to a corner, and climb up by cracks and grooves to the top of the Tower.

73 **Rotten Chimney** 150 ft. Difficult
H. I. Ogilvy and N. P. Piercey, 20 June, 1940.

This is the chimney which lies some 40 ft. along the Western Traverse. Climbed in two pitches, it is steep, exposed and well named.

Douglas Boulder

The following routes all ascend the rocks of the Douglas Boulder.

74   East Gully   500 ft.   Easy

This is the gully followed to the Douglas Gap on the Ordinary Route. Easy scrambling throughout. *Diagram, p. 104.*

75   East Ridge   200 ft.   Difficult

J. H. B. Bell and R. G. Napier,   6 April, 1896.

Climb as for the Ordinary Route to the point where the East Gully begins to be defined. A large grass ledge leads to the right, traverse this 30 ft. then climb steep but easy rock 90 ft. to belay in a square corner. Climb this and a similar corner above in two pitches of 20 ft. each. Easier rocks lead to the top of the boulder in 60 ft. *Diagram, p. 104.*

75a   Variation   60 ft.   Very Difficult

J. Y. MacDonald and H. W. Turnbull,   17 March, 1931.

Climb a vertical corner from within the East Gully. *Diagram, p. 104.*

76   Direct Route   700 ft.   Very Difficult

William Brown, L. Hinxman, H. Raeburn and W. Douglas, 3 April, 1896.

Start at the lowest rocks, a little left of a smooth slab wall, which is an obvious feature of the lower section of the face.

Climb easily by a shallow groove for 150 ft. to a point where the groove steepens to form an open chimney. Climb this for 200 ft. to gain a well defined ledge. Traverse this to the right, climb steep but broken rock to the top of the boulder. Belays are small but sufficient throughout. *Diagram,* p. 102.

77 **Direct Route II**   600 ft.   Severe

D. Browning and H. Small.

Start under the right edge of the smooth slab wall which is a prominent characteristic of the lower rocks of the Boulder.

Climb the slab just right of a sickle scoop to the terrace above; scramble to the foot of the steep upper section which is then climbed direct. The crux is at the top of the wall where easier rock is gained from the top of a leaning block. Continue more easily to the top of the Boulder. *Diagram,* p. 102.

78 **North-west Face**   600 ft.   Difficult

W. G. McClymont and J. H. B. Bell,   10 May, 1936.

As viewed from the hut a feature of the North-west Face are three chimneys in the form of an inverted 'N'. The original route is climbed to the base of these chimneys and then follows the central chimney.

Start to the right of the smooth slab wall, a prominent feature of the lower rocks. Climb an easy angled groove to a short wall barring access to the left-hand chimney, 150 ft. Climb the wall to enter the chimney, 20 ft. Follow the chimney for 20 ft., then traverse slabs rightwards to gain the central diagonal chimney, 60 ft. Follow the chimney to its final section which narrows and contains a chockstone. Some 20 ft. below this chockstone traverse slabs onto the rib on the right, then climb up and left to finish at the

chimney exit, 80 ft. A choice of routes then leads to the top
of the Boulder, 150 ft. *Diagram*, p. 102.

79 **Left Hand Chimney**   310 ft.   Difficult

B. P. Kellett,   21 June, 1944.

Start as for the North-west Face and climb to the base of
the left hand chimney. The chimney is continued beyond
the point where the first party traversed into the central
chimney. Climb a series of short pitches to reach a large
ledge, 160 ft. The line of the chimney continues above the
ledge and this is followed to the summit of the Boulder,
150 ft. *Diagram*, p. 102.

80 **Right Hand Chimney**   500 ft.   Severe

B. P. Kellett,   18 July, 1944.

Start in a small bay directly under the right hand
chimney of the inverted 'N' and climb easy rocks to the
foot of the chimney, 150 ft.

Surmount the first overhang by bridging; climb to belay
on the left edge, 50 ft. Continue up the chimney, turn an
overhang by the rib on the right and climb to a recess, exit
left and climb slabs to belay at the right end of a large ledge,
120 ft. Easier climbing by choice of routes leads to the summit
of the Boulder, 150 ft. Dry conditions are recommended.
Diagram, p. 102.

81 **Cutlass**   400 ft.   Very Severe

E. Cairns and F. Harper,   6 July, 1963.

This route follows the clean cut corner which lies some
100 ft. left of the South-west arête of the Douglas Boulder.

Climb by easy slabs 130 ft. to a flake belay, move up into
the corner, belay, 30 ft. Climb the corner to a ledge and

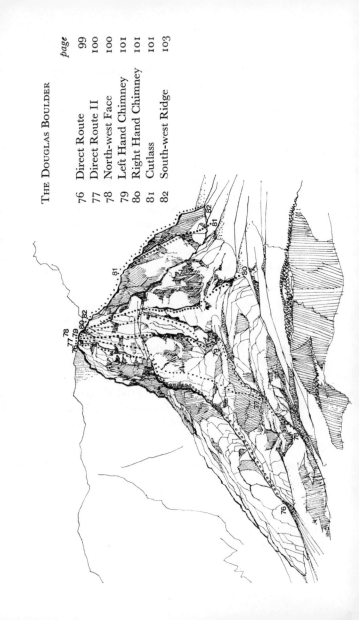

belay on the right wall, 100 ft. Continue by the chimney above, 70 ft. A further 70 ft. gives access to the South-west ridge. *Diagrams*, pp. 102, 120.

82 **South-west Ridge**   500 ft.   Moderate

J. W. Burns, W. A. Morrison, W. C. Newbigging and A. E. Robertson,   4 August, 1904.

The route follows the crest of the well defined ridge overlooking West Gully and is the easiest of the face routes to the top of the Douglas Boulder. *Diagrams*, pp. 102, 120.

83 **West Gully**   450 ft.   Easy

The West Gully leads to the Douglas Gap and, while slightly steeper, it is more direct than the East Gully when approaching from the C.I.C. Hut. *Diagram*, p. 120.

WINTER   I

The gully is a straightforward ascent on snow. The traverse of the gap i.e. up West and down East Gully, provides an interesting expedition.

EAST FLANK OF TOWER RIDGE

G   Great Tower
L   Little Tower
D   Douglas Boulder
e   Echo Wall

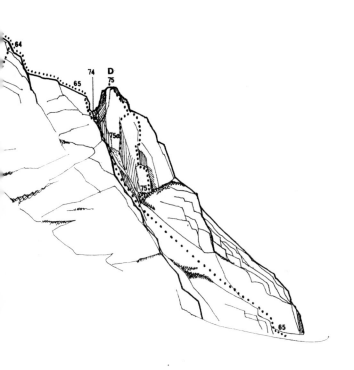

Secondary Tower Ridge

The Secondary Tower Ridge lies on the West flank of Tower Ridge and some distance below its crest taking the form of a slanting shelf, parallel to the main ridge and separated from it by a well-defined depression which holds snow till late in the season.

For the most part it hardly attains the status of a distinct ridge. At its upper extremity it rises steeply to the top of the pinnacle buttress of the Tower to terminate just below and to the West of the Great Tower.

84 **1934 Route**   600 ft.   Moderate
J. Y. Macdonald and H. W. Turnbull,   26 March, 1934.

Start 150 ft. to the right of West Gully. Climb by a wide shallow gully for 150 ft., then traverse right into a slabby groove which is climbed for 150 ft. followed by scrambling to reach a point situated above Vanishing Gully. Follow the crest for 300 ft., then traverse left to gain the crest of Tower Ridge below the Little Tower. *Diagram*, p. 120.

WINTER   II

Climb snow to the slabby groove which often carries ice and presents the only real difficulty. Thereafter follow the snow shelf to the upper reaches of the Tower Ridge, where a selection of routes either up or down can be made.

85 **1931 Route**   400 ft.   Difficult
20 March, 1931.

Some 300 ft. further along the West flank of Tower Ridge, in a bay formed by a steep projecting buttress, twin chimneys lead up to the crest of the Secondary Tower Ridge. The 1931 Route uses the right hand of these.

Climb to a belay on the left wall, 25 ft., continue up the chimney under a chockstone generally using the left wall to reach a platform at 60 ft. The chimney now opens out to become a groove and this is followed with little difficulty in pitches of 50, 100 and 100 ft. to reach the 1934 Route which is then crossed to gain the shallow gully dividing the Secondary Tower Ridge from the Tower Ridge. *Diagram*, p. 120.

WINTER   III

Climb steep snow into the chimney which is then followed, normally over three short ice pitches, to reach the easier upper snows of the 1934 Route. A choice of routes can thereafter be taken, up or down.

85a   **Variation**   170 ft.   Difficult
B. P. Kellett,   19 June, 1943.

This follows the left hand of the cleft twin chimneys.

Climb the chimney 50 ft. to belay. Continue up the chimney moving onto the left wall to avoid the overhang above, belay a few feet above, 60 ft. Climb the steep rib on the left to gain the groove of the 1934 Route, 60 ft.

85b   **Variation**   90 ft.   Severe
I. S. Clough,   18 April, 1959.

This follows the steep rib which divides the twin chimneys, starting at the foot of the right hand chimney.

86   **Beggar's Groove**   600 ft.   Very Difficult
*I. S. Clough, J. Pickering, C. Anderson, R. Henson, P. Brocklehurst
    and R. Porteous*,   20 May, 1959.

Start half-way between the 1934 Route of the Secondary

Tower Ridge and the foot of the narrow hanging gully to
the right (Vanishing Gully).

Climb a chimney to a grass ledge and belay, 50 ft. Follow
the groove above to a large block (runner), step down right,
traverse up right along a groove to a stance and probable
chockstone belay, low down, 100 ft. Cross a groove, climb
a wall leftwards then up to a platform above the lower
tier of slabs, 80 ft. A cairn here marks a junction with
Vagabond's Rib. The route now follows the grooves and
cracks above to gain the crest of Tower Ridge (as for Vagabond's Rib), 300 ft. *Diagram*, p. 120.

87 **Vagabond's Rib**   650 ft.   Severe
I. S. Clough,   18 April, 1959.

Start 220 ft. to the right of the West Gully directly below
steep slabs bounded on the right by a hanging gully
(Vanishing Gully).

Climb easily to a belay centrally placed below the slab,
50 ft. Climb the slab to a niche and belay, 80 ft., move out
right and climb the steep crest by a groove and crack to
belays, 60 ft. Continue more easily by the slabs ahead to
reach the crest of Tower Ridge in 300 ft. *Diagram*, p. 120.

88 **Lady's Day**   360 ft.   Very Difficult
I. S. Clough, C. MacInnes and E. Buckley,   18 April, 1959.

Start 30 ft. right of Vagabond's Rib and immediately
left of Vanishing Gully. All pitches are of 60 ft. Climb to a
stance, traverse right across the gully then up to a stance,
peg belay. Climb a steep slab above then trend rightwards
to spike belay. Traverse up rightwards to gain the groove
of the 1934 Route. *Diagram*, p. 120.

VANISHING GULLY

This is the conspicuous gully which drains the lower part of Secondary Tower Ridge. The top part is deep and wide, but lower down it narrows to a crack and finally disappears.

89 **Vanishing Gully**   350 ft.   IV

R. Marshall and G. Tiso,   15 January, 1961.

Under normal conditions the gully presents an ice fall over the first 200 ft.

On this ascent an ice cave was gained at 40 ft. then a bulging ice wall climbed to easier ground 60 ft. higher. Another steep ice pitch, 60 ft., then left to the easier upper reaches and a junction with the Secondary Tower Ridge. *Diagram*, p. 120.

90 **Rogue's Rib**   650 ft.   Severe

T. W. Patey and J. Smith,   1 April, 1956.

This is the name given to the steep two-tiered buttress which projects from the West flank of Tower Ridge just beyond the chimneys of the 1934 Route. On the first ascent the steep lower pitches were avoided by the gully on the right which was then snow and ice filled. Shortly after, K. Bryan and N. Harthill ascended from the lowest rocks and continued by the original route 150 ft. higher to make the first complete ascent.

Start immediately left of the gully (The Italian Climb) which bounds the buttress on its right.

Climb the crest 70 ft. to a belay then by the right flank to a large platform, 100 ft. Continue up the shallow chimney above for 90 ft. to gain easier climbing which leads in 200 ft. to the base of the upper tier of the buttress. Climb by thin cracks for 30 ft. then traverse left into the obvious chimney to belay at 60 ft. Follow the chimney to some huge perched blocks, traverse right, climb up behind a large flake to reach a chockstone belay, 80 ft. Continue by the chimney above, or the ridge on the right to the top of the Buttress, 100 ft. *Diagram*, p. 120.

WINTER   IV

I. S. Clough and G. Grandison,   2 January, 1960.

On this ascent the line of the original ascent was taken and followed throughout. 7 hours.

91   **The Italian Climb**   600 ft.   Severe

B. P. Kellett,   24 July, 1943.

This is the name given to the deeply cut gully which defines the right flank of the steep two tiered buttress of the Rogue's Rib. The gully starts abruptly. Climb 30 ft. to a shallow cave and belay. Bridge out over the roof to reach easier climbing in 30 ft. A stretch of scree leads to the next cave pitch. Climb the steep rib on the right for 25 ft., traverse left and make a long stride. Regain the chimney on the right by an awkward swing across a smooth slab. Above the chimney take the shallow right hand branch of the gully which leads to the crest of the ridge just below the Little Tower of Tower Ridge. *Diagram*, p. 120.

WINTER   IV

J. R. Marshall, A. McCorquodale and G. J. Ritchie,   January 1958.

The first chimney presents an ice groove leading into the cave, the exit from which is very difficult. Snow then leads to the upper chimney which presents a very steep ice pitch about 30 ft. high with, under normal conditions, the rock projecting to enable bridging up over the cave. The upper section of the gully trends right at an easier angle by snow slopes and occasional ice pitches to the crest of Tower Ridge. Under well banked up conditions, the entrance pitch becomes a short ice wall. Allow 3–4 hours for the ascent to the crest of the ridge.

92 **The Chute**   750 ft.   IV

J. R. Marshall, R. N. Campbell and R. Holt, February 1965.

About 100 ft. right of the Italian Climb a line of grooves are seen to lead directly up the face. On the first ascent a rising traverse left then right was made to gain entry to the grooves above the extremely steep entry pitch.

Start under the grooves then make a rising traverse leftward, 100 ft. Climb into an ice groove on the right and climb 40 ft. to a ledge leading horizontally across a steep wall which leads to a small gully, 110 ft. Move out right by a rising traverse on rock and ice to reach a stance below a steep ice wall, 100 ft. Climb the ice, 80 ft., then by a snow gully for 200 ft. to the base of a steep rock buttress. Follow an easy snow shelf rightwards to reach the top of Broad Gully, 200 ft. Finish down this and then up Tower Ridge. Allow 4–8 hours for the ascent. *Diagram,* p. 120.

93 **Ruritarian Climb**   750 ft.   Severe

C.U.M.C. party, Mid 1950s.

Start just right of the Italian Climb and climb easily to a large block belay, 100 ft. Move up rightwards to cross a chimney groove to a stance and belay, 100 ft. Continue obliquely by clean slabs to Broad Gully, 250 ft. Across the gully climb by a selective line to the foot of the Great Tower, 300 ft. *Diagram,* p. 120.

Garadh na Ciste

Beyond Italian Climb the main flank of Tower Ridge is separated from the Coire na Ciste by a deeply cut gully (Garadh Gully). To the right of the gully is a small buttress crowned by a spacious platform. This is Garadh na Ciste, so named for its resemblance to a 'Jardin' in the Alps.

94 **Garadh Gully** 300 ft. III
I. S. Clough and M. Bucke, 16 February, 1958.

This is the deeply cut gully which leads from the foot of Italian climb to Garadh na Ciste.

Under normal conditions the gully gives a straightforward climb with two steep ice pitches some 50 ft. each. *Diagram,* p. 120.

95 **East Ridge of Garadh na Ciste** 300 ft.
Moderate
G. Graham Macphee, G. C. Williams and P. Ghiglione, 8 October, 1933.

Climb the crest of the buttress just to the right of Garadh Gully. *Diagram,* p. 120.

The following routes on the West flank of Tower Ridge are gained from the Garadh na Ciste.

96 **Broad Gully** 300 ft. Easy
B. P. Kellett, 24 July, 1943.

From the top of Garadh na Ciste a raking scree gully leads up leftwards across the face, under the Pinnacle Buttress to join the Secondary Tower Ridge. Continue beyond this with little difficulty, to gain the crest of Tower Ridge, just below the Little Tower. *Diagram,* p. 120.

WINTER   II

I. S. Clough and M. Bucke,   16 February, 1958.

The summer route was followed to the Secondary Tower
Ridge. A descent of 100 ft. was then made and a short gully
climbed to gain the main ridge below the Little Tower.

97   **Pinnacle Buttress of the Tower**   500 ft.
                                                   Difficult

G. T. Glover and W. Inglis Clark,   28 June, 1902.

Start about 150 ft. up Broad Gully. Climb a corner and
crack, steep but with good holds, 70 ft., belay. Easier ground
trending up rightwards leads to a broad ledge, 60 ft. This
if followed continues on into Tower Gap West Chimney
however quit the ledge under the steep upper prow of the
buttress to climb by a rightwards raking groove, 100 ft.
Move up left by a chimney groove to reach a ledge above
the prow of the buttress, 40 ft. Traverse left into a groove,
leading through slabs to easier ground, 100 ft. Now follow
the crest of the ridge to the foot of Great Tower, 100 ft.

The above description probably gives the best line of
ascent, but many variations are possible both left and right
of the crest of the buttress. *Diagram,* p. 120.

WINTER   III

D. J. Bennet and A. Tait,   17 November, 1957.

The ascent went by the rocks to the right of the buttress.
From the top of the Garadh na Ciste follow Broad Gully
until a ledge can be followed raking up rightwards for some
250 ft., to a point a little beyond the steep crest of the upper
section of the buttress.

Climb by a snow filled groove 60 ft., traverse right 40 ft.
to another groove which is followed to easier rocks leading
leftwards onto the top of the buttress below the Great

Tower. A selection of routes thereafter leads to the summit plateau (see Tower Ridge).

98 Glover's Chimney (Tower Gap West Chimney)
450 ft. Very Difficult

G. T. Glover, Dr. and Mrs. Inglis Clark, 27 June, 1902.

The climb starts from the Garadh na Ciste and goes directly by the narrow gully to Tower Gap. The lowest rocks are overhanging and, under normal conditions, wet.

Climb for a short distance by an ill defined ledge which rakes steeply up rightwards to gain the right wall. Surmount a short steep section of rather smooth rock then, by a traverse back left, regain the gully bed some 200 ft. above the start. Continue up the gully by a series of short easy pitches to the final chimney which is climbed by bridging well out to finish by the right wall or by climbing the chimney direct to the Tower Gap (a more difficult variation). *Diagram,* p. 120.

WINTER III

G. Graham Macphee, G. C. Williams and D. Henderson, 17 March, 1935.

Under normal conditions the lower rocks are masked by a great ice fall, which involves about 100 ft. of step cutting on steep ice followed by some 30 ft. of snow to gain a stance. Mixed snow and ice climbing leads back left into the gully which is then followed, mainly on steep snow, to the final chimney. This can be climbed by either the right or left walls to gain the gap. Allow 3–5 hours for the ascent.

99 Goodeve's Route Moderate

T. E. Goodeve, C. Inglis Clark and J. H. A. McIntyre, 28 December, 1907.

This climb was the result of a successful attempt by the members of a belated party to escape off Tower Ridge.

From the Great Tower make a descending traverse to the right (or West) to reach Glover's Chimney. Cross the Gully and continue the traverse by a ledge rightwards to a wide recess which holds snow till late in the summer. From this recess climb a chimney on the left, then an exposed rib of rock followed by several easy chimneys and short pitches which lead to the summit plateau. Beyond the recess considerable variation is possible. If the traverse is continued beyond the recess the upper part of Raeburn's Easy Route can be gained.

This area of the precipice carries a thick covering of snow in the winter months.

100   **The Gutter**   300 ft.   Difficult
C. G. M. Slessor, G. Waldie and S. Paterson,   3 October, 1954.

From a point about half way up Glover's Chimney, where the ledge of Goodeve's Route crosses the gully take the rocks on the right wall. Climb by ribs and grooves on rough rock to the plateau, belays as required.

101   **Raeburn's Easy Route**   350 ft.   Easy
H. Raeburn and A. W. Russell,   28 September, 1911.

Start above and to the right of Garadh na Ciste about 200 ft. to the left of Number Two Gully.

Traverse upward to the left until an easy staircase leads to a ledge sloping up and back to the right for a short distance. Easy scrambling leads left again to a wide sloping ledge below the final steep wall. Follow the ledge to the right for a considerable distance to finish up a well-defined gully giving access to the summit plateau about midway between the top of Number Two Gully and the Tower Ridge. *Diagram*, p. 120.

S.M.C. Party, names not recorded (See S.M.C.J. 15.332),
   April 1920.

A thick covering of snow and ice completely alters the
character of this climb.

From near the foot of Number Two Gully traverse left
under a steep wall to a large ice fall. Climb this, 100 ft. of
step cutting may be required to gain a snow slope leading
upwards to a long traverse to the right below the final wall,
which is turned by steep snow at the far end. Gain the
plateau by the easiest route over the cornice which is not
normally heavy at this point.

Number Two Gully Buttress

Beyond the rather indeterminate wall of Raeburn's Easy
Route is a scimitar shaped buttress defined on its right by a
deeply cut gully (Number Two Gully). This is Number
Two Gully Buttress. The lower third is set at a low angle
with only the upper section giving continuous climbing.

102 **Number Two Gully Buttress**   400 ft.
                                                    Very Difficult

J. D. B. Wilson and G. A. Collie,   2 August, 1947.

   Start at the lowest point of the buttress to the left of
Number Two Gully. Two moderate pitches, separated by
scrambling, lead in 150 ft. to a rock rib overlooking the
gully and abutting onto the steepening of the buttress above,
stance and belay. Traverse the corner on the left into an
open groove, climb this on sloping holds to belay, 45 ft.
Continue up the crest by steep exposed pitches of 50, 30
and 30 ft. Finish by scrambling, 100 ft. *Diagram,* p. 120.

WINTER   III

J. R. Marshall, L. S. Lovat and A. H. Hendry,   23 March, 1958.

   Mixed rock and ice at an easy angle lead to a large snowfield under the steepening of the buttress. About 60 ft.
left of the crest of the buttress, climb a steep ice groove 70 ft.,
then by mixed snow and ice trend rightwards to reach the
crest of the buttress a few feet below the summit plateau.
Allow 2–5 hours.

III

*I. S. Clough, N. Stebbing, P. Cresswell, W. Reid, N. Bull and
    D. Ducker,* 1 April, 1960.

On this ascent the summer route was followed throughout
with the groove pitch proving the crux. This is generally
the more difficult line in winter. Allow 2–5 hours.

103 **Number Two Gully**   400 ft.   Very Severe

B. P. Kellett and J. A. Dunster, 30 August, 1942.

This is the large, deeply cut gully to the right of Number
Two Gully Buttress and the indeterminate rocks extending
from Tower Ridge.

The rocks of the gully can rarely be dry. Parties are
recommended only to attempt the ascent following a spell
of dry weather when the volume of water will be reduced to
a less formidable hazard.

Follow the gully without serious difficulty to the foot of
the Great Pitch, 100 ft. This is an overhung groove. Wet and
extremely difficult, it is best climbed by back and foot,
facing left. At 30 ft. easier climbing gives access to scree
which is followed to a chockstone belay at 100 ft. Continue
by two short pitches above to finish, 100 ft.

Parties ascending the gully should take care to ensure
following members of the rope take adequate shelter from
falling stones as the gully screes are very unstable. *Diagram,*
p. 120.

WINTER   II

J. Collier, G. Hastings and W. C. Slingsby, Good Friday, 1896.

The gully fills up well and normally presents a steep
uncomplicated snow slope sometimes interrupted by a
short ice pitch at the narrows. The cornice is occasionally
large, and could be difficult to surmount.

COMB GULLY BUTTRESS

This is the wedge shaped buttress to the right of Number
Two Gully. A narrow easy angled crest leads to the broad
middle section topped by a steep rampart. The right flank
is defined by the narrow, twisting, Comb Gully.

104 **Comb Gully Buttress**   450 ft.   Very Difficult

B. P. Kellett, July 1943.

Start at the lowest part of the buttress. Climb to the foot
of a 'V' chimney, 90 ft. Continue by the rocks on the left to
follow the crest overlooking Comb Gully, 100 ft. A short
awkward chimney then some loose rocks lead to the easy
angled centre section of the buttress.

This point can be gained easily from near the foot of
Number Two Gully and was the route by which the first
ascent was made. Climb the upper section of the buttress
by an easy angled chimney on the left to reach a broad
ledge, 100 ft. The line of the chimney continues above as
a groove. Climb this in two pitches of 60 and 80 ft. to the
plateau. *Diagram*, p. 120.

WINTER   III

I. S. Clough and J. M. Alexander,   8 January, 1960.

The central snow field was gained from Number Two
Gully and ascended to follow a groove on the left edge of
the buttress. From the groove make a rising traverse rightward to the foot of a prominent curving chimney in the steep
final rocks. Climb the chimney then trend left to gain the
plateau.

105 **Comb Gully**   450 ft.   Severe

I. S. Clough and J. M. Alexander,   29 June, 1958.

Climb the gully by scree and some short pitches for 300 ft.

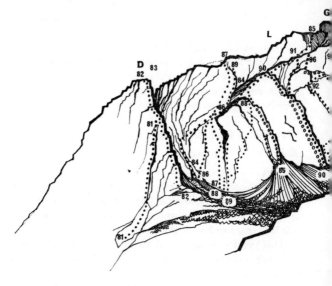

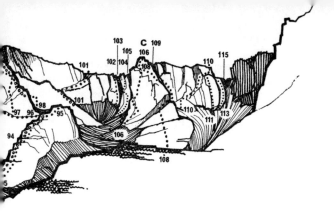

to the foot of the steep upper section of the gully. Climb the next pitch, first by the right wall, cross the water course and finish by the left wall to reach a chockstone, 35 ft. Climb by back and foot to avoid a greasy overhanging chockstone to stance and belay in the gully bed, 30 ft. Continue to a small cave under a chockstone; make a strenuous exit over this to take a peg belay, 30 ft. Climb the groove 10 ft. then by the right wall to pass the overhanging capstone, 40 ft., block belay. Continue by the groove on the left to reach the gully bed, 10 ft. Scrambling leads to the plateau. *Diagram,* p. 120.

WINTER   IV

F. G. Stangle, R. Morsley and P. A. Small,   12 April, 1938.

Under normal conditions a steep snow slope leads to the upper section. This presents four ice pitches each surpassing in difficulty as height is gained. The first pitch is climbed by the left wall, the middle pitches by bridging and the final one on the right wall, by what is sometimes an awkward ice bulge.

Under heavy snow conditions the pitches become almost obliterated by snow, at which times it provides a straightforward ascent much reduced in difficulty.

The lower slopes of this gully have a tendency to avalanche. Parties attempting the ascent should take extra care when such conditions prevail on the mountain.

Comb Buttress

This buttress dominates the Southerly regions of Coire na Ciste as a great wedge, girdled at one-third height by a raking ledge rising from left to right. On each flank steep gullies define the buttress, to the East, Comb Gully and to the West, Green Gully which separates the Comb from Number Three Gully Buttress. Below the raking ledge the buttress is easy angled and slabby, whereas the upper tier is protected for most of its Northerly length by considerable overhangs, forcing recorded lines of ascent on to the Eastern and Western flanks of the buttress.

106 **Tower Face of the Comb**   700 ft.

Very Difficult

H. I. Ogilvy, C. F. Rolland and J. R. Hewitt, June 1940.

From the left end of the raking ledge, which splits the buttress about one third of its height, move up the screes 100 ft. to the highest of the slabby ledges which run parallel to the main ledge.

Traverse the ledge rightwards to near its termination, 80 ft., belay. Climb the steep slabs on the left to a large platform encumbered with shattered blocks, 80 ft., belay. Gain the obvious groove above and climb by its left edge till at 40 ft. a steep section forces a left traverse to gain easier climbing and a flake belay, 60 ft. Climb more easily for 80 ft. to reach a grassy groove which is then followed to the base of a steep wall, 80 ft. Traverse right to a large ledge with a high flake forming a window at the right hand end. Climb over the window and round a corner on the right to

stance and belay, 90 ft. Continue by the crest of the buttress
to the summit plateau, 350 ft. *Diagram*, p. 120.

106a   **Variation**   150 ft.   Very Difficult

G. Dwyer and J. H. B. Bell,   6 August, 1940.

From the flake belay above the third pitch traverse
rightward to enter a long chimney which leads to a junction
with the flake and window of the original route.

106b   **Variation**   150 ft.   Severe

B. P. Kellett,   18 July, 1943.

Traverse as above to take a line up the steep wall between
the original route and the chimney variation.

106c   **Variation**   200 ft.   Severe

J. R. Marshall and J. Stenhouse,   July 1958.

From the base of the steep wall follow a groove up leftwards by moss bolsters and occasional rock to join Hesperides
Ledge at midpoint. Finish by that route.

WINTER   Very Severe, IV

R. Smith and R. Holt,   1 January, 1959.

With minor deviations, the summer route can be followed
throughout.

The lower section presents sustained climbing over very
steep rock and ice with little respite until the central snow
filled grooves are reached. Above these, some short but
awkward walls provide serious difficulties before the crest
is gained. The crest of the buttress, though easier, can
absorb much time, particularly in conditions of high wind
or deep powder snow. Under most conditions the winter
ascent is a serious expedition. Allow 4–7 hours.

107   **Hesperides Ledge**   200 ft.   Very Difficult

J. H. B. Bell and J. D. B. Wilson,   16 June, 1940.

Climb Comb Gully some 300 ft., then move out onto the

right wall by a steeply inclined, curving shelf, which is 'a perfect garden of mossy and lush vegetation'.

There are several difficult corners to negotiate before the crest of the buttress is gained about 300 ft. below the summit plateau. Poor rock.

WINTER   III

J. R. Marshall, J. Stenhouse and D. Haston,   12 February, 1959.

The difficult corners remain and present exposed step cutting. The crest of the buttress is equally difficult at a further two points and may consume much time. On the first ascent the climb was found to be Very Difficult in standard. Allow 3–5 hours.

108 **Pigott's Route**   800 ft.   Severe

A. S. Pigott and J. Wilding,   24 September, 1921.

Start at the lowest point on the Northerly side of the buttress. Climb by a chimney, 80 ft., then easy rocks to gain the raking ledge 200 ft. above the start. Follow the ledge rightwards to near its Westerly termination in Green Gully, to a point a few feet beyond a large block. Climb the under-cut, flake-chimney above to reach a grass stance and belay, 30 ft. Continue directly by steep slabs and ribs to a grass ledge, 70 ft., belay. Easier climbing leads to the crest of the buttress which is followed, with fine situations, to the summit plateau, 350 ft. *Diagram*, p. 120.

WINTER   IV

J. R. Marshall and R. Smith,   12 February, 1960.

The lower section was avoided and the raking ledge followed on hard snow to the base of the flake-chimney. This was very difficult and ice filled. Above the chimney a traverse left was made for 30 ft. to enter a steep ice filled groove which was climbed to the crest of the buttress. A sustained climb on steep ice, allow $3\frac{1}{2}$ to 7 hours.

109   **Green Gully**   400 ft.   Very Difficult

D. Pipes and I. S. Clough,   6 July, 1958.

Climb steep rocks immediately to the right of the water course for 80 ft. to the easy bed of the gully which is then followed to the steep section above. This is climbed direct; the rock is somewhat loose but good protection is available, 80 ft. Continue for 120 ft. to the final steep section which is turned on the left wall in 70 ft. Scrambling then leads to the plateau. *Diagram,* p. 120.

WINTER   IV

J. H B. Bell, J. Henson, R. Morsley and P. A. Small,   4 April, 1938.

The lower rocks are masked by a steep banking of snow from which a steep 40 ft. wall of ice leads to the easy ground of the traverse ledge. Above, two short ice pitches lead to another steep ice pitch about 60 ft. high; this sometimes presents an awkward ice bulge best climbed from right to left. Snow then leads to the final difficulties which can present another steep pitch, bulging in its upper reaches.

A fairly sustained climb on steep ice with little natural protection. Allow 3–6 hours for the ascent.

Number Three Gully Buttress

Adjoining Green Gully on its right a slab wall extends to abut the main mass of the buttress which presents a steep impressive face overlooking Lochan na Ciste and Number Three Gully further to the right.

110 **Number Three Gully Buttress**   400 ft.
                                          Moderate

H. Raeburn, Dr. and Mrs. Inglis Clark,   29 June, 1903.

Start up the easy rocks to the right of Green Gully to gain the foot of a long groove raking up to the right, 80 ft. Follow the groove for 150 ft. to reach a large corner above which a steep chimney crack rises. Traverse right then up by steep but easy rocks to arrive at a large platform, 20 ft. Climb up to a smaller platform, 20 ft. Traverse rightwards to gain an obvious ledge leading across the upper face of the buttress, 100 ft. From the termination of the ledge climb by slabby rock to the plateau, 20 ft. *Diagram*, p. 120.

110a **Variation**   110 ft.   Very Difficult

From the smaller platform climb up to the left to belays, near the foot of a well defined chimney, 50 ft. Climb the chimney which is steep and exposed with loose rock in the lower section then, by a recess above, climb to the plateau, 60 ft.

WINTER   III

L. Lovat and D. Bennet,   18 February, 1957.

Climb to gain a snow shelf raking up to the right, then

from the highest point, traverse right by a steep ice and snow section to gain the large platform. On the original ascent the chimney variation was followed. This normally provides climbing on steep ice in two pitches of 30 ft. and 40 ft. to finish.

If the original summer line is followed, climb to gain the obvious traversing ledge leading across the face and follow this to a stance at the far end. An iced slab then leads to the top of the buttress.

Both these lines of ascent are in exposed situations. Allow 2–4 hours for the ascent.

111   **The Knuckleduster**   400 ft.   Very Severe

J. R. Marshall and R. Marshall,   4 September, 1966.

This route ascends the great groove which is an obvious feature of the steep face of the buttress overlooking Lochan na Ciste.

Climb the groove to belay under the overhang, 130 ft. Continue, to turn the overhang by a slab on the right, belay on the outer edge, 50 ft. Regain the groove by a horizontal ledge, continue by a crack in the right wall to belay, 120 ft. Climb the wall on the right to gain the large platform of the original route, 100 ft. *Diagram*, p. 120.

112   **Thompson's Route**   360 ft.   Difficult

S. and B. P. Thompson,   23 September, 1941.

Start from the foot of Number Three Gully and follow the chimney bounding the right flank of the very steep front of the buttress.

Climb the chimney 40 ft. to the left end of a well-defined ledge (this point can be gained by walking from further up the Gully). Continue by the chimney in pitches of 40, 60 and 60 ft. to easier climbing which leads leftwards to the 'large platform' of the Ordinary Route, 100 ft. From the small platform above climb up directly to finish by a square corner to the right of the chimney variation of the Ordinary Route.

WINTER   III

R. Marshall, J. R. Marshall and J. Stenhouse,   December 1963.

The summer line was followed throughout. Continuous ice climbing was required on the first 3 pitches, thereafter the difficulties lessened. Allow 3 to 4 hours for the ascent.

113   **Gargoyle Wall**   400 ft.   Very Difficult

*W. Peascod, B. L. Dodson, C. Peckett, J. Renwick and G. G. Macphee,*28 August, 1950.

The Gargoyle is well seen on the righthand skyline from the descent of Number Three Gully. Start 30 ft. right of the chimney of Thompson's Route on the ledge which cuts across the top of the first pitch.

Climb the steep wall above by a zigzag route to a well-defined ledge, 70 ft, belay. Descend slightly from the left hand end of the ledge to enter the first chimney which is climbed, surmounting a large chockstone to gain a rocky bay level with the Gargoyle now visible on the right, 70 ft. Traverse to the Gargoyle, crossing the groove then a short gangway, onto the head, 30 ft. Climb the ridge above, past a perched block to a ledge, traverse right into a corner, belay, 40 ft. Climb the corner to a stance and block belay below a steep wall, 20 ft. Continue by the steep crack above to a rock platform and belays, 30 ft. Traverse 20 ft. left to a chimney crack which is climbed on good holds to a stance and belay, 60 ft. Continue up the chimney with more difficulty, 20 ft. (This section can be avoided on the left).

The continuation of the chimney is followed more easily to the top of the buttress, 20 ft. *Diagram*, p 120.

114   **Winter Chimney**   300 ft.   III

D. Haston and D. Gray,   March 1963.

This route ascends the chimney lying in the back of the bay which defines the right edge of Gargoyle Wall. Start 100 ft. up the gully from that route.

The chimney contains 3, sometimes 4 short ice pitches and can provide a sustained ascent on steep ice. Allow 4 hours for the ascent.

115   **Number Three Gully**   300 ft.   Easy

This gully is situated centrally at the back of Coire na Ciste and separates Number Three Gully Buttress from Craig Coire na Ciste. It is a straightforward ascent on scree with a scramble on loose rock of some 30 ft. to finish.

The gully is easily identified by a pinnacle standing as a flat topped blade of rock at the head of the gully. This feature is a useful identification characteristic in locating the gully from the mist shrouded plateau. The descent should be started to the right of this pinnacle. *Diagrams*, pp. 120, 136.

WINTER   I

In winter a uniform snow slope fills the gully. The cornice can be large, but there is normally an easy break formed to the right of the pinnacle.

The gully is much used as a quick means of descent. After the first 20 or 30 ft., which are often icy, the gully provides an uncomplicated descent to the Lochan na Ciste.

Creag Coire na Ciste

The buttress is contained by the Number Three and Four Gullies. It comprises a series of minor buttresses and gullies of considerable steepness.

116 **South Gully**   400 ft.   II

G. G. Macphee, 10 April, 1936.

Start from the foot of the narrow section of Number Three Gully, level with the lowest rocks of Number Three Gully Buttress.

Climb an obvious slanting ledge leading rightwards to the foot of a steep gully which turns back up to the left. Under heavy snow it can be a straightforward climb, normally there are two ice pitches varying from 20 to 30 ft.

In some seasons the cornice will be large. Allow 2 to 3 hours. *Diagram,* p. 136.

117 **Central Gully**   400 ft.   III

I. S. Clough and J. M. Alexander, 28 January, 1959.

This ascent follows a line just left of the Central Rib. Start at the lowest rocks and climb by a series of snow patches left of the rib to the foot of two parallel ice gullies, 220 ft. Climb the leftmost gully on steep ice; this is strenuous but good protection can be obtained, 120 ft., peg belay. Cross into the right-hand gully and climb on snow to the plateau. In some winters the final cornice can be formidable. *Diagram,* p. 136.

117a **Variation**   120 ft.   IV

I. MacEacheran and J. Knight.

On this ascent the right-hand branch was climbed through-out. It provided a sustained and difficult climb on high angle ice. Allow 3–4 hours for the complete ascent.

118 **Central Rib**   400 ft.   Difficult

M. W. Erlebach and E. C. Pyatt,   10 July, 1941.

Start at the lowest point of the crag; climb by a rock rib in a series of short pitches to where the rib steepens and becomes well defined, 220 ft. Continue by the left edge overlooking a narrow chimney gully, 170 ft. This section terminates on a ledge which leads easily leftwards under the final tower to the plateau. *Diagram*, p. 136.

118a **Variation**   50 ft.   Very Difficult

B. P. Kellet,   10 July, 1943.

Climb the tower by rightward slanting grooves to the left of the two obvious cracks. *Diagram*, p. 136.

119 **Wendigo**   350 ft.   IV

T. W. Patey and J. Brown,   24 February, 1963.

Start in the bay to the right of Central Rib. Ascend a steep rake of rock and ice slanting rightwards up the steep buttress overlooking North Gully which lies to the right.

The climb involved two 100 ft. pitches of sustained difficulty, giving access to a snow bay just under the plateau. The climb should be at least severe, allow 3 to 4 hours. *Diagram*, p. 136.

120 **North Gully**   350 ft.   Very Difficult

G. G. Macphee and A. G. Murray,   29 September, 1935.

Start half-way between the lowest rocks of Creag Coire na

Ciste and the narrows of Number Four Gully beneath a steep waterworn groove. Climb by the bed of the gully to a small recess and belay, 60 ft. The gully narrows and steepens, continue using the left wall and the bed of the gully to gain easier ground, 40 ft. The route now skirts the steep upper rocks by easy slabs leading rightwards to a narrow slanting gully which gives access to the plateau, 200 ft. *Diagram*, p. 136.

WINTER   II

J. Y. Macdonald and H. W. Turnbull,   24 March, 1934.

The foot of the gully is masked by steep snow which leads to the narrowing of the gully. There is, under normal conditions, a 40 ft. ice pitch, which can be vertical or even bulging for some 10 to 15 ft. The route is then followed to the right over easier snow and ice to the plateau. The cornice is rarely difficult.

In lean snow years the ice pitch can be longer and more difficult. Allow 2–4 hours for the ascent.

121   **North Gully—Left Fork**   120 ft.   III
D. Bathgate, J. Knight and A. McKeith,   February 1964.

From the snow basin near the top of North Gully climb up left into a steepening snow scoop, then up a steep, narrow iced groove at its back on the right to the cornice and plateau. *Diagram*, p. 136.

122   **Number Four Gully**   300 ft.   Easy
This gully separates Creag Coire na Ciste from the rock mass of the Trident Buttresses. Above the great scree slopes beyond the Lochan na Ciste Number Four Gully trends to the right, partially hidden behind the South Trident Buttress and gains the plateau at the lowest point between Ben Nevis and Càrn Dearg 3961. The ascent is over unstable screes with no pitches. *Diagrams*, pp. 136, 144.

The gully provides a straightforward snow climb and probably the easiest line of descent from the plateau.

123 **Number Four Gully Buttress** 400 ft.
Moderate

J. H. B. Bell and R. B. Elton, 1 January, 1929.

Start to the right of the narrows of Number Four Gully a short distance above the wide ledge leading out right onto the South Trident Buttress.

Climb by a leftward raking chimney groove to easier ground, 200 ft. Continue over rock and scree to the steeper final rocks which can be climbed at several points to reach the summit, 150 ft. *Diagrams,* pp. 136, 144.

South Trident Buttress

This is the most Southerly and best defined of the Trident Buttresses. It is sharply bounded on the North or right by the gully of the Central Trident Route and on the left by Number Four Gully with its attendant screes.

The buttress comprises three tiers, the lowest is steep with the routes on it leading to the upper reaches of a broad grassy ledge. This point can be gained easily from the screes under Number Four Gully. The middle tier commences above the ledge and is defined above by a similar though smaller ledge raking up from the narrows of Number Four Gully. The final tier is a narrow shattered ridge providing scrambling to the summit screes.

124   **1934 Route**   320 ft.   Very Difficult
G. G. Macphee and G. C. Williams,   24 June, 1934.

Start at the lowest point of the buttress. Climb to a dark corner below a rotten chimney, 50 ft. Descending slightly, traverse left round the rib to gain a shallow gully, 30 ft., belays. A few feet up this gully climb the right wall to a stance and belay, 50 ft. Continue over large blocks to a well defined ledge, 50 ft. From the left end of the ledge climb a bulge to gain slabs which lead to the foot of a clean cut corner, 90 ft. Traverse left and up to reach the top of the first tier, 50 ft.   *Diagram*, p. 144.

124a   **Variation**   50 ft.   Severe
A. B. Black and A. Swan,   12 June, 1954.

Climb the crack at the back of the clean cut corner to finish at the top of the first tier.

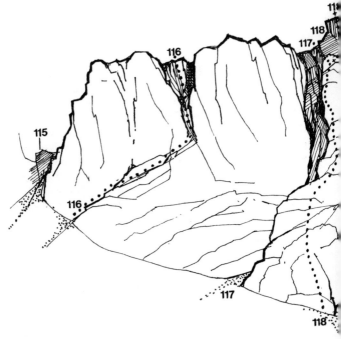

CREAG COIRE NA CISTE

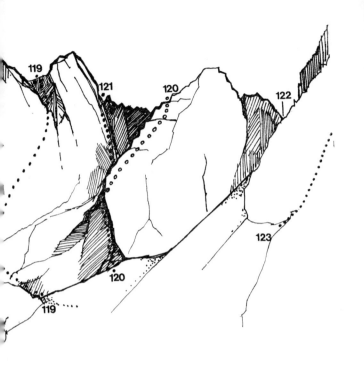

125   **1936 Route**   350 ft.   Severe

W. G. McClymont and J. H. B. Bell,   10 May, 1936.

Start to the left of the lowest rocks. Climb up on the left
of a shallow gully cross the gully at 40 ft. and climb the steep
rocks above to stance and belay, 50 ft. Continue for 20 ft.
then traverse rightwards by a series of shelves to reach a
grassy ledge and block belay. Above the block, climb up
to the right on steep rock to reach the foot of an obvious
groove which is climbed to the top of the first tier, 140 ft.
Diagram, p. 144.

126   **1944 Route**   400 ft.   Severe

B. P. Kellett,   30 July, 1944.

Scramble to the foot of the steep wall at a point about
100 ft. right of the 1934 Route.

Climb left of the steep chimney then trend left to a ledge
and belay, 80 ft. Climb from a large, leaning block, to the
foot of the second groove from the left; traverse right under
the third groove to a point beneath the fourth and rightmost groove, 80 ft., belay. Climb into the groove then, using
a crack in the right wall, reach a system of ledges which
are followed to a steep corner, 110 ft. Finish by the corner
in 40 ft. to gain the middle ledge near its Northern termination. *Diagram,* p. 144.

> The following routes ascend the middle tier of the
> buttress and can be approached either by the lower
> routes or by traversing the terrace from the screes
> of Number Four Gully.

127   **The Groove Climb**   250 ft.   Very Difficult

B. P. Kellett,   25 June, 1943.

Above the left end of the screes under the middle tier

is a deep chimney groove, easily identified by a small pinnacle at its exit.

Climb the groove to a deep cave, belay, 100 ft. Make an awkward exit then up to belays, 30 ft. Continue up to the right by easy cracked slabs to reach the crest of the buttress, 120 ft. *Diagram*, p. 144.

128 **Sidewinder**   320 ft.   Very Severe

J. R. Marshall, R. Marshall and A. Wightman, June 1964.

The route is on the South face of the middle tier of the buttress. Look for a triple tiered corner rising steeply leftwards across the face and starting about 50 ft. to the right of an obvious flake chimney. (The Groove Climb).

Scramble from the ledge to the foot of the corner, 75 ft., belay. Climb the corner by cracks in three pitches of 50, 30 and 70 ft. to gain an easy slab. Continue directly above by the line of the crack and a large flake to gain the crest of the buttress below the final tier, 100 ft. *Diagram*, p. 144.

129 **Spartacus**   320 ft.   Very Severe

I. S. Clough and G. Grandison, 12 June, 1962.

Start from the ledge under the rocks of the middle tier, traverse beneath the arête right of Sidewinder to the foot of a corner. This is 60 ft. left of the great corner, a major feature of this tier of the buttress.

Climb the corner, surmount the overhang, then traverse right to stance and peg belay, 90 ft. Follow a little groove on the right to a flake, descend a few feet, cross the steep wall to an arête, then climb to large flake belay, 50 ft. Continue directly then left above the overhang to a flake crack. Follow this for a few feet then traverse right to belays on an arête, 80 ft. Climb the groove above to gain the top of the middle tier, 100 ft. *Diagram*, p. 144.

130   **The Slab Climb**   300 ft.   Very Difficult

B. P. Kellett,   30 July, 1944.

Start midway between Spartacus and the great corner.

Climb the right hand of two cracks to an overhang,
traverse into the left crack to stance and belay, 80 ft. Continue by the crack to a conspicuous chimney, belay, 80 ft.
Climb the chimney, strenuous, 50 ft. The chimney can be
avoided on the left. Follow the continuation of the chimney
to the top of the middle tier, 90 feet. *Diagram,* p. 144.

131   **The Clanger**   300 ft.   Severe

J. R. Marshall and J. Stenhouse,   June 1964.

This route ascends the chimney groove at the back of the
great corner.

Gain the groove from the right to reach a belay at 70 ft.
Continue up the groove to a steep cave pitch, 120 ft., belay.
Follow the chimney in two steep sections to the final bay,
exit to the right on steep rotten rock, 100 ft. *Diagram,* p. 144.

WINTER   IV

J. R. Marshall, R. Marshall and R. N. Campbell,   March 1967.

Sustained difficulties on rock and ice led to the steep cave
pitch, thereafter an escape was made by the right wall where
a through route for thin men leads behind a large flake onto
the crest of the buttress. Allow 3–4 hours for the ascent.

132   **Pinnacle Arête**   500 ft.   Very Difficult

H. Raeburn and Dr. and Mrs. Inglis Clark,   29 June, 1902.

Start up from the rightmost termination of the middle
ledge at a point overlooking the steep North wall of the
buttress.

Climb sloping ledges for 10 ft. then an awkward corner

on the right, followed by 30 ft. of difficult rock to reach easier ground. Trend left onto the crest and climb to the foot of a steep wall; climb this direct on good holds or by joining the chimney crack about mid-height on the left. A further short steep section gives access to the narrow shattered crest leading to the final tier of the buttress which consists of scrambling to the summit plateau. *Diagram*, p. 144.

WINTER   IV

R. H. Sellars and J. Smith,   February 1959.

Follow a snow traverse across the middle ledge then, by a series of snow and ice grooves immediately right of the crest, reach the easier upper section of the buttress. Allow 2–4 hours for the ascent.

Central Trident Buttress

This is the indeterminate mass of rock lying to the right of Central Gully. It comprises several minor buttresses and gullies extending Northwards to merge with the rocks of the North Trident Buttress.

133   **Central Gully**   800 ft.   Very Difficult

G. G. Macphee.

Start at the foot of the gully which defines the right or Northern flank of the South Trident Buttress and lies almost directly above Lochan na Ciste.

Climb scree and enter the left fork at the bifurcation, one or two short pitches lead to a vertical rib of rock, usually wet. Take the left wall and climb to a steeply sloping ledge, then up left to an exposed platform. Continue round the corner then break up rightwards to a grassy platform. Traverse the slab above to the right to gain easy ground. Scramble 200 ft. to the foot of the upper buttress. This is climbed on steep rocks up the centre of the face to a pinnacle where two awkward moves above lead to a short steep wall climbed on good holds to gain easier climbing leading to the summit. *Diagram*, p. 144.

WINTER   III

H. Raeburn, Mrs. W. Inglis Clark and C. Inglis Clark, April 1904.

In winter the gully fills up well. Normally snow, interrupted by one short ice pitch, leads to the steep ice column well seen from below. The original party turned this on the left by mixed snow and ice to regain the upper snow bay at the earliest opportunity. The steep upper buttress was turned on the left by a gully, then regained above the steep section and followed to the summit.

VARIATION   IV

L. S. Lovat and K. Bryan,   11 March, 1956.

The steep ice column was climbed direct.

134 **Jubilee Climb**   850 ft.   Very Difficult

G. G. Macphee, G. C. Williams and D. Henderson,   5 May, 1935.

From the bifurcation in the lower reaches of Central Gully take the shallow right-hand branch over easy slabs and scree for 250 ft. to below a steep corner and crack. Climb this 10 ft., traverse right over blocks to belay. Climb the slabs above, 40 ft. then scree for 40 ft. to a short chimney and slab which lead in 100 ft. to a scree slope.

The upper buttress can be seen higher up on the left, gain the base and climb by the crest of the buttress in two steep pitches, 240 ft. Scrambling leads to the final slope of Càrn Dearg 3961. *Diagram, p. 144.*

135 **Jubilation**   700 ft.   IV

R. Marshall, J. R. Marshall and J. Stenhouse,   December 1963.

Climb the Jubilee Route to the 10 ft. pitch. Traverse left into twin chimneys and climb the right-hand branch on steep ice to a snow bay, 60 ft. Regain the left branch and climb 80 ft. on ice to easier chimneys which are followed for several hundred feet to the final arête of the buttress. Time taken 4 hours. *Diagram, p. 144.*

SOUTH AND CENTRAL TRIDENT BUTTRESSES

North Trident Buttress

The rocks of this buttress form the Northern or rightmost edge of the main mass of the Trident Buttresses.

Easy angled rocks at the base lead to steep twin ridges separated by a gully. These ridges can also be reached by the steep face of rock further left along the base of the buttress.

136 **Neptune Gully**   500 ft.   III

A. J. Bennet and J. Clarkson,   15 February, 1956.

This is the gully which splits the Northern or right-hand crest of the buttress. It lies to the left of the original route.

Climb the snow slopes covering the lower rocks of the original route to an ice pitch barring access into the gully. Turn this on the right then climb a short pitch to gain the foot of a steep ice pitch. This is turned by the left wall to a ledge then, by a hard corner, regain the gully. The next pitch is turned by the ice bound rocks on the left; thereafter snow leads between steep buttresses to a 25 ft. pitch climbed direct to reach snow slopes leading to the large platform overlooking Number Five Gully. Continue by the easy ridge and slopes above to the plateau. Allow 3–5 hours for the ascent.

137 **North Trident Buttress**   500 ft.

Very Difficult

The route ascends the indefinite rocks on the right edge of the buttress, defined on the right by Moonlight Gully.

Start by the rocks of a trap dyke and climb without difficulty to a broad ledge, 150 ft. Trend left to climb the right-hand ridge leading to the foot of the final tower,

250 ft. Climb the steep exposed edge, 70 ft. Beyond the scree above the final rocks provide moderate climbing. *Diagram,* p. 152.

WINTER   IV

J. Maclay, H. Raeburn, C. W. Walker and H. Walker, 1 January, 1904.

The lower rocks are generally masked in snow, thereafter the difficulties are fairly continuous by mixed climbing to the final tower. This may be climbable direct but can be extremely difficult, otherwise the tower can be turned with less difficulty to gain the upper section of the buttress. This leads with less difficulty to the summit. Allow 3–5 hours.

137a **Variation: Direct Start**   150 ft.   Severe

G. G. Macphee, J. Jackson Murray, D. J. S. Harvey, 1 May, 1935.

Start about midway along the base of the steep section of rock to the left of the original route.

Climb into a well-defined corner to belays, 30 ft. Continue by the corner to thread belay and cave recess, 80 ft. Cross the slab wall on the right to a wide ledge and easier climbing above. The original route can be rejoined by traversing to the right, alternatively continue up the gully above to finish by a wall and ridge leading onto the final section of the original route.

WINTER   III

D. Haston and party.

A steep cone of snow leads into the upper corner pitches. Climb steep ice for 30 ft. to the easier slopes leading to the upper rocks.

138   **Moonlight Gully**   500 ft.   I

W. Inglis Clark and T. Gibson,   3 January, 1898.

The gully lies to the right of North Trident Buttress and separates it from Moonlight Gully Buttress which lies to the right.

The gully is narrow and straight and ends in the wide upper funnel of Number Five Gully. A steep snow climb. Allow 2 to 3 hours under normal conditions. *Diagram,* p. 152.

Moonlight Gully Buttress

This is the two-tiered section of rock which lies between Moonlight Gully and the lower reaches of Number Five Gully.

139 **Diagonal Route**   300 ft.   Moderate

I. H. Ogilvie and J. Ward,   1 August, 1936.

Start at the foot of Moonlight Gully and make a right-ward ascending traverse to a broad terrace. Continue by the leftmost of two chimneys to the top of the first tier. Climb the upper tier by the continuation of the chimney. *Diagram,* p. 152.

140 **Right Hand Chimney**   400 ft.
                                                    Very Difficult

G. Scott, E. M. Hanlon and B. P. Kellett,   25 July, 1943.

Start midway between the gullies, at the foot of the right-most and better defined of the chimneys splitting the buttress. The route follows the chimney throughout and is steep and sustained for 200 ft. Thereafter easier climbing leads to the top of the first tier. Climb with little difficulty by the continuation of the chimney in the upper tier, 100 ft. *Diagram,* p. 152.

141 **Number Five Gully**   1500 ft.   Easy

This is the gully separating the Trident Buttresses from the Great Buttress of Càrn Dearg. It is a wide shallow gully opening out to become virtually a corrie in its upper reaches.

A rib of rock divides the gully, the left branch is drier and easier; higher up a large chockstone is passed by a through route. If this is too wet a rib on the left can be climbed. In the upper section the true gully trends up to the right between rock ribs leading almost to the summit of Càrn Dearg. *Diagrams*, pp. 152, 170.

WINTER   I

The summer pitches can present short ice pitches otherwise the climb is on snow. Cornices can be massive above the gully but the rim is extensive and an easy exit should always be available.

Care should be exercised under avalanche conditions.

Number Five Gully Buttress

This is a steep exposure of rock which stands some half-way up the right flank of Number Five Gully.

Above the lower narrows of the gully, a broad scree ledge leads out rightwards into a bay under the North wall of the buttress and a short exposure of rock which extends out to the North.

142 **Fives Wall**   200 ft.   Severe

J. R. Marshall and C. L. Donaldson,   September, 1953.

Half-way up the Number Five Gully face of the buttress is a curving grass ledge, follow this to the far end to a cairn marking the start of the route.

Climb a groove to a ledge, traverse right beyond its termination then up to a large flake. Climb this, then cracks to reach a large slab ledge. Traverse left, climb a short crack and wall to a large ledge. Further right a steep crack gives access to the top of the buttress. *Diagram*, p. 152.

143 **The Slant**   450 ft.   Very Severe

T. Sullivan and N. Collingham,   19 September, 1959.

Start at the lowest point of the buttress. Climb up to the left to a ledge with block belays, 50 ft. Continue by awkward corners, gain a gangway at the top, step right and then left to belay below a cracked slab, 120 ft. Climb the slab then traverse right to a small corner, 50 ft. Break out left, traverse left up a slab then trend leftwards up a steep wall to reach a large ledge, 130 ft. Scrambling leads to the top of the buttress, 100 ft. *Diagram*, p. 152.

144 **The Twist** 470 ft. Very Severe

I. S. Clough and G. Grandison, 14 June, 1962.

The climb uses the gangway of the Slant (direct), traverses to the edge of the buttress, then continues by the easiest line to the top.

Start at the lowest rocks, under a steep corner. Climb a short steep groove to a ledge (foot of the gangway) and continue to a peg belay under a little corner crack, 40 ft. Climb the crack, combined tactics or otherwise, then up to a spike belay, 40 ft. Climb to the top of the gangway, move right, then left to reach the stance and belay below the cracked slab (as for Slant), 50 ft. Traverse right to gain sloping ledges above the overhanging wall, belays, 40 ft. Climb diagonally rightwards over a big flake, then horizontally, by sloping shelves to a peg belay under an obvious corner, 60 ft. Climb the corner to a block belay, 50 ft. Traverse right, then up to a chockstone belay by a pinnacle, 65 ft. Follow the cracks above to the top of a huge pedestal block, chockstone belay, 50 ft. Gain the ledge above, climb into a groove on the left, then out right to a large block; finish up left to reach a grass ledge, 75 ft. Scrambling now leads to the top of the buttress. *Diagram,* p. 152.

145 **The Chicken Run** 500 ft. Very Severe

J. R. Marshall and J. Stenhouse, 30 May, 1961.

Start 150 ft. up right from the lowest rocks of the buttress. Climb a steep crack to a ledge, 90 ft. Continue slightly rightwards on shattered rock to an obvious rock ledge, 40 ft. Traverse this leftwards to gain a great flake, 50 ft. Climb the wall above to a ledge, 40 ft. Follow a series of cracks and awkward corners to a larger ledge. A relenting angle leads in 200 ft. to the top of the buttress. *Diagram,* p. 152.

Number Five Gully Buttress

146 **Turkish** 590 ft. Very Severe

J. Ferguson and C. Higgins, June 1967.

The route ascends the left wall of the great corner which dominates the Northern face of the buttress.

Climb a prominent wide crack, below and to the left of the corner then move left over short walls to belay on a ramp at twin pegs (just before the left traverse of Chicken Run), 130 ft. Move up the ramp, surmount an awkward corner then onto the foot of the great corner, 120 ft. Climb the left wall leftwards to gain large, loose blocks then, using a peg, tension left 10 ft. to a ledge. Continue directly to a platform and belay, 100 ft. Move left, ascend a short steep wall then, by scrambling, ascend a short gully, 120 ft. Continue to the foot of the final wall then bear hard right for 100 ft. to belay on the crest of the buttress, 120 ft. *Diagram,* p. 152.

147 **Fives Gully** 120 ft. Very Difficult

I. S. Clough, 10 February, 1959.

This is the small gully separating the main buttress from a small steep face leading out to the North. The gully holds little snow in winter and the ascent is by very shattered rock. *Diagram,* p. 152.

148 **Crack and Chimney** 120 ft. Very Difficult

I. S. Clough and P. Nicolson, 8 April, 1958.

Start 75 ft. right of Fives Gully at the foot of a crack leading up to a chimney.

Climb the crack to belay below the chimney. Gain the chimney, awkward, then more easily to finish. *Diagram,* p. 152.

149   **Easy Chimney**   120 ft.   Moderate

B. P. Kellett, R. L. Plackett and O. M. Plackett.

Start 150 ft. right of Fives Gully.

The route follows the twin chimney cracks lying at the back of a recess which is almost a gully, poor rock. *Diagram*, p. 152.

WINTER   II

I. S. Clough,   10 February, 1959.

Steep snow and occasional rock. Allow $1\frac{1}{2}$ hours for the ascent.

150   **Ledge Route**   Easy

J. S. Napier, R. G. Napier and E. W. Green,   9 June, 1895.

Start up Number Five Gully, break out right on to the third ledge from the foot of the gully and follow this till it becomes impracticable. A shallow gully then leads up left to a higher ledge which is again followed to the right. This eventually leads to the easy angled crest of the Great Buttress and to a platform on which a large cairn has been erected. Follow the crest above to the summit plateau. *Diagram*, p. 152.

WINTER   II

Under normal conditions the route provides an interesting ascent, on snow throughout. Allow $1\frac{1}{2}$–$2\frac{1}{2}$ hours for the ascent.

Càrn Dearg Buttress

This buttress lies to the right of Number Five Gully. When viewed from the C.I.C. Hut the buttress presents a magnificent face of overlapping slabs and great overhangs, probably unmatched anywhere in the country. The right-hand or Northern flank of the buttress returns in an impressively steep wall to a junction with Waterfall Gully.

151 **Mourning Slab**   350 ft.   Very Severe

I. S. Clough and K. Sutcliffe,   1 June, 1961.

Start at the foot of the big slab corner 100 ft. left of Route I. Climb into the corner and continue to stance and belays, 70 ft. Traverse to the arête then climb to a small stance and poor belays, peg, 50 ft. Move to the overhanging corner which is normally wet, traverse right then up moving leftwards above the roof to reach a scoop leading to a good ledge and belays, 70 ft. Round the corner to enter a groove then climb to a grass ledge from where scrambling leads to the Ledge Route, 130 ft. *Diagrams*, pp. 152, 170.

WINTER   V

J. Knight and D. Bathgate,   February 1965.

A great cataract of ice develops over the length of this route which has become known as the 'Curtain'. The ascent is by continuous cutting on steep ice and is a regular 'Tour de Force'.

Climb on ice the great introductory slab, to a stance and peg belay under the final ice wall. Using pegs, surmount

the wall near its left edge to gain the easy slopes of Ledge
Route. Time taken on the first ascent, 6½ hours.

152   **Route I**   700 ft.   Very Difficult
*A. T. Hargreaves, G. Graham Macphee and H. V. Hughes,
    17 June, 1931.*

Start to the left of the lowest rocks of the minor, curving
buttress which lies on the lower left flank of the buttress.

Climb to a ledge and belay, 45 ft. Follow the right edge
to a big ledge, 60 ft., then scramble by grassy cracks to the
left to reach a large block belay 30 ft. above. Traverse left
below a groove till a good stance and belay are gained at
the foot of a slab, 20 ft. Climb into the groove and follow
this to a recess, 40 ft., belay. Continue up to the right then
left to a platform and belay, 40 ft. Scrambling leads to the
top of the minor buttress.

Walk right to the foot of an obvious chimney, climb this
finishing by a grassy groove to a recess and belay at 70 ft.
Climb the right wall 20 ft. to a belay, 10 ft. above regain the
chimney and climb to a stance and spike belay at 50 ft.
Move out left, climb an exposed slab to a belay at the foot
of the final chimney, 25 ft. Climb the chimney to a broad
ledge at 40 ft. Walk right then climb easier rocks to gain
the Ledge Route, 150 ft. *Diagram*, p. 170.

152a   **Variation, Direct Start**   Very Difficult
R. L. Plackett and W. W. Campbell,   31 August, 1941.

Start at the lowest rocks of the minor buttress and climb
by the right edge, then by a groove on its right wall to join
Route I. *Diagram*, p. 170.

153   **P.M.**   600 ft.   Very Severe
G. Farquhar and I. S. Clough,   21 September, 1966.

Follow the variation start to Route I to the cairn at the

top. On the left, about half-way between the Route I chimney
and the corner of Mourning Slab, a leftwards move round a
bulge leads to a groove which is climbed (peg runner) to a
grass ledge below a slab corner, 40 ft. Trend left across the
slab, then up left to cross an overlap and reach a stance and
chock belay at some flakes, 120 ft. Up and cross the slab on
the right to a grassy stance and thread belay, 50 ft. Climb
a steep grassy crack for 20 ft. then right across slabs to the
'spike belay' of Route I, 50 ft. Go right to climb a bulging
corner and the crack above to the top, 80 ft. *Diagram*,
p. 170.

154 **Route II**   500 ft.   Severe

B. P. Kellett and W. A. Russell,   9 June, 1943.

Climb Route I to the foot of the chimney section above
the minor buttress. Climb the chimney for 40 ft., traverse
the slab on the right to a small stance and good belay, 20 ft.
Make up right in two pitches of 30 and 50 ft. to reach a large
flake beneath the great overhangs. Climb above the flake,
traverse lush, loose vegetation to a platform with an inconspicuous thread belay low down, 40 ft. This section is better
climbed by traversing the flake for 20 ft. then ascending a rock
rib to the thread belay. Traverse across the buttress to the right
in two pitches of 100 and 30 ft. to gain a platform on the
edge of the buttress. Scramble up the edge of the buttress
100 ft., then enter a groove which is followed mainly on the
right wall for two pitches of 70 and 40 ft. to gain the crest
of the buttress. *Diagram*, p. 170.

154a **Variation, Direct Start**   250 ft.   Severe

B. W. Robertson and G. Chisholm,   19 May, 1962.

Start at a cairn on a grass ledge to the right of the lowest
rocks of Route I. Climb the centre of a smooth slab to a small
ledge traverse, 4 ft. right to a wall then by a small slanting

corner to traverse left to a stance. Finish by a small black crack to a flake belay, 100 ft. Continue straight up to a large block below a groove, 50 ft. Climb the groove then traverse round an arête on the right to gain a shattered ledge, 30 ft. Continue by the bulge above to reach easier ground and a small belay near the chimney of Route I, 80 ft. *Diagram*, p. 170.

155 **The Shadow**   800 ft.   Very Severe

T. Sullivan and N. Collingham,   19 September, 1959.

Start a few feet right of the direct start to Route II at the foot of a thin crack.

Climb the crack then traverse right to belay, 90 ft. Surmount the block above, round a corner then follow a little groove to a grass ledge, 40 ft., belay. Climb the wall above, step right to enter a grassy groove, 90 ft. Follow the groove until it widens then traverse 30 ft. right to block belays, 120 ft. Climb up then traverse left below a black slab to break through the overlap; continue to a small corner, 130 ft. Make an ascending right traverse across a wet streak to the grassy groove of Centurion, 130 ft. Then climb up right to belay in a grassy corner on the crest of the buttress, 120 ft. Climb the right wall of the corner, then traverse left across another slab to a ledge, belay, 80 ft. Finish by the groove above, 80 ft. *Diagram*, p. 170.

156 **The Bullroar**   800 ft.   Very Severe

J. R. Marshall and J. Stenhouse,   30 May, 1961.

This is a rising traverse across the face of the buttress. Start 100 ft. to the right of Route I, at some large boulders, climb up into a groove, peg, then to a flake belay, 90 ft. Then move up left into a parallel groove which is followed to a belay, 50 ft. Traverse the slabs rightward, under the lap to reach a crack, climb this to belays, 45 ft. Descend and continue the traverse to a stance and peg belay, 50 ft. Continue the traverse, ascending, to gain the belay above pitch 3 of Centurion, 100 ft. Climb the crack above then traverse right to stance and peg belay, 90 ft. Move rightwards then up to reach the terrace above the chimneys of The Bat and Sassenach, 100 ft. From the left end of the terrace traverse to an area of shattered rocks beneath an undercut groove, 40 ft. Climb the groove and continue above by a series of corners and slabby grooves to the top of the buttress, 400 ft. *Diagram*, p. 170.

VARIATION   50 ft.   Very Severe
J. McLean and W. Smith,   June 1962.

From the flake belay above the first pitch continue directly by the groove, avoid the left traverse, surmount the bulge above and climb to the belay, 50 ft.

157 **Torro**   700 ft.   Very Severe
J. McLean, W. Smith and W. Gordon,   25 July, 1962.

Start just left of the foot of the rib which forms the left wall of Centurion's corner, about 100 ft. right of the Bullroar. Climb an overhanging groove with the aid of a peg, continue to a flake runner. Climb the groove above to a large flake, ascend the right-hand side, move back left and continue up a groove to a good stance and large flake belay, 100 ft. Climb a widening fault then a bulge on the left to the edge of the slab, peg runner. Traverse left across the slab, step round the corner then go up an overhanging groove to good stance and flake belay, 80 ft. Climb diagonally right round a bulge to enter a crack, climb this for 20 ft., move slightly right then up slab to good stance and peg belay, 80 ft. Climb a slight crack 25 ft., step left onto a higher slab, peg runner. Move across the slab 8 ft., climb the overhang above trending leftwards (peg) finishing by the groove above in 20 ft., to a good stance, peg belay, 70 ft. Climb the fault for 15 ft., traverse the slab rightwards to a crack, follow this to an overhang which is climbed trending leftwards then finish by a groove to reach a grassy stance, peg belay, 140 ft. Continue up a fault to a grass ledge beneath large overhangs, peg belay, 100 ft. Climb up into a large scoop, move left-wards onto a steep slab, continue diagonally leftwards to gain a large block, thread runner. An awkward move left on good holds leads to a steep slab, continue up rightwards for 40 ft. to a good stance and peg belay, 110 ft. Traverse left to a large corner, climb into this (peg) and continue to grass terrace. *Diagram*, p. 170.

158 **Centurion** 650 ft. Very Severe
D. D. Whillans and R. O. Downes, 30 August, 1956.

This route follows the great central groove which is a prominent feature of the lower reaches of the buttress.

Start at the undercut base of the groove and climb the left wall to a large platform, move right to enter the groove and climb to a ledge and belays, 50 ft. Continue by the corner, which affords good protection, to a slab stance in an overhung bay, 120 ft. Traverse left onto the edge, follow easy grooves, step right onto the lip of a big overhang, then climb up to stance and peg belay, 80 ft. Move back into the corner, traverse left up the wall below the overhanging crack then follow the arête to a stance, 70 ft. Climb slabby grooves by the same line, to a small stance and block belay, 70 ft. Continue by the same line then move leftwards to the stance before the long traverse pitch of Route II, 60 ft. Climb up to the overhang, traverse left to a slab. Move left up to another overhang, then step from a detached flake to traverse delicately up left on to a large slab. Climb this

easily up to the right to stance and belay below the second
tier of overhangs, 90 ft. Traverse right 20 ft., then climb a
spiky arête to a bulge, above which step left into an easy
groove leading to a broad ledge, 80 ft. *Diagram*, p. 170.

159   **King Kong**   1000 ft.   Very Severe

B. W. Robertson, F. Harper and J. Graham, 1 and 2 September,
    1964.

Climb the first pitch of Centurion. Traverse out right on
the slabs at 20 ft. rope down to a lower slab 10 ft., then
traverse rightwards to a peg belay under an open corner,
70 ft., 3 pegs. Climb the corner (peg) gain a sloping slab,
then up to a corner (junction with the Bat). Make a descending traverse left, past the block belay to the big loose block,
peg belay, 110 ft. Climb up left over a slab to a jug-handle
on the first overlap. Climb this then traverse right to climb
a chockstone crack on the second overlap. From the slab
above, descend rightward, then up to a small ledge under a
smooth groove, move slightly left and up then slightly right
to a point just below a bulge. Swing right into a scoop to a
peg belay, 90 ft., 4 pegs. Take the line left, then up to a
huge overlap. Climb an 8 ft. overlap just to the right then
traverse right to a sloping ledge below a vertical crack.
Climb this, 15 ft. to a small ledge, peg belay, 60 ft. Continue
by the crack, to follow an easy rightward traverse. From its
end, climb an arête, then slightly left to a smooth slab and
peg belay, 90 ft. (just left of the belay at the top of the 100 ft.
corner of the Bat). Traverse left over a slab, climb a wide
crack to a small overlap, climb this and follow the crack in
the upper slab to a large overlap (peg below), Climb the
overlap direct. Follow the slab above and slightly right, to
the large overlap, climb this by a crack (wedge) then by
slabs and an easy broken overlap climb up left to a small

grassy ledge, peg belay on right, 130 ft. (1 peg and wedge).

Climb easily by a grassy bay to a vertical wall, traverse left and up to a block belay below an overhanging wall, capped by a small roof, 60 ft. Climb the wall by a crack then using slings, surmount the overhang. Above, move left then up a slab corner, heading for a huge roof, to a peg belay below an overhanging corner, 130 ft., 1 wedge. Climb the corner, swing across to a spike, move left then up to a spike and stance, 130 ft. Move slightly right then up to a grassy groove, move left then up to finish, 100 ft., cairn. *Diagram*, p. 170.

160   **The Bat**   1000 ft.   Very Severe
D. Haston and R. Smith,   September 1959.

Climb the first pitch of Centurion, 50 ft. Enter the corner, at 30 ft. traverse out right by slabs to a large block then, by the shelf, continue rightwards to a block belay, 110 ft. Descend 10 ft. then move up and right by a shelf, into a corner, over a short wall to a triangular slab. Follow the V-groove above then by slabs trend rightward to belay under the Sassenach chimney, 90 ft. Turn the edge on the left, then climb a short groove to gain the corner above, 40 ft. Climb the corner direct, pegs and sling or none, 100 ft. Follow the groove to the left end of a terrace, 110 ft. Move right and climb into an undercut groove (just above the Sassenach chimney) 110 ft. Continue by the line of the grooves above, belays as required, 400 ft. *Diagram*, p. 170.

161   **Sassenach**   800 ft.   Very Severe
J. Brown and D. D. Whillans,   18 April, 1954.

Start below and to the right of the great chimney corner at a point where a large slab of rock leans against the face.

From just left of the slab, climb sloping mossy ledges for

20 ft., until it is possible to step right onto a nose. Traverse
left to the foot of a crack and climb this to stance and belay,
110 ft. Climb the corner above with the aid of slings to the
overhang then traverse left and up beneath the overhang to
belays at the foot of the great corner, 90 ft. Climb the chimney
to a grassy terrace, 170 ft. Move up and rightwards by the
terrace to the foot of a 'V' groove, capped by an overhang,
60 ft. Climb the groove for 30 ft., step out left onto a ledge.
Continue by the crack above to enter another groove, 110 ft.
Climb the groove to step right at the top, 40 ft. Enter the
grooves above which continue in 300 ft. to the top of the
buttress. *Diagram*, p. 170.

161a **Variation**   250 ft.   Severe

T. W. Patey, W. Brooker and W. Smith,   1953.

The foot of the chimney was gained by a traverse from
Waterfall Gully across Titan's Wall to a ledge which leads
at the same level into the base of the chimney. *Diagram*, p. 170.

162 **Titan's Wall**   370 ft.   Very Severe

I. S. Clough and H. MacInnes,   19 April, 1959.

This route follows a line of cracks on the vertical North
wall of the buttress and is dependent on peg climbing over
the greater part of the ascent.

Start 40 ft. along the foot of the North wall, climb by
cracks (peg runners) to an overhang at 50 ft. Using pegs
follow the crack line trending right to a ledge. Traverse
this to the left until above the overhang, peg belay, 120 ft.
Return along the ledge to rejoin the crack line, continue on
pegs over bulges to a ledge and belay, 150 ft. Climb up
to the left then right to enter a groove (peg runner) which is
followed to a junction with the upper pitches of Sassenach,

100 ft. Finish by that route to the top of the buttress, 450 ft. *Diagram*, p. 184.

163 **The Shield** 350 ft. Very Severe
D. D. Whillans and R. O. Downes, 1 September, 1956.

The North wall of the buttress is defined by Waterfall Gully. Above the huge introductory pitch of this gully an enormous flake stands against the North Wall, forming a chimney. This is the line of the route.

Climb as for Evening Wall to gain Waterfall Gully, 80 ft. Cross the gully, scramble to a broad glacis, then descend grass to the foot of the chimney, 150 ft. Climb the chimney, awkward, to a small grass ledge, 60 ft. Follow the chimney until it is possible to step left to a small cave, thread belay, 40 ft. Regain the chimney, surmount a difficult bulge and continue to a belay, 130 ft. Continue by the line of the chimney, becoming grassy, to gain the top of the flake, 120 ft. This is a junction with the upper pitches of the Evening Wall Route which is now followed to the top of the buttress, 160 ft. *Diagram*, p. 184.

163a **Variation: Direct Start** 220 ft. Very Severe
J. R. Marshall, R. Marshall and G. J. Ritchie, June 1962.

Start at the foot of the North wall of the buttress, 20 ft. right of Titan's Wall and a few feet left of the deep cut cracks of the corner.

Climb the wall 15 ft., traverse right into the crack and climb to belays, 80 ft. Follow the crack, a few feet under the great roof; move on to the left wall then, with the aid of pegs, climb a thin crack to surmount the left edge of the roof. From the stance above climb a short chimney to stance and belay, 50 ft. Continue by the line of the chimney to a block belay, 60 ft. Climb the steep groove above, traverse right to join The Shield above the first chimney pitch, 60 ft. (As for Orgy). *Diagram*, p. 184.

164 Evening Wall   700 ft.   Very Difficult

C. F. Rolland and H. I. Ogilvy,   19 June, 1940.

Climb a clean cut chimney 30 ft. right of the foot of Waterfall Gully. Exit by the left wall and climb to a block belay, 80 ft. Continue above for 20 ft. then cross the gully on the left, climb the far wall by a difficult edge, followed by slabs to gain grass, 100 ft. Climb an easy angled chimney 50 ft. then a rightward trending groove on the wall above to reach the raking slabs which lead up to the base of an enormous flake, 120 ft. Continue by a chimney to the top of the flake, 30 ft. Traverse left over grass and easy rock to a flake belay, 100 ft. Gain the crest of the buttress; climb up leftwards then make a short traverse right and up to gain a large ledge, 70 ft. Move left along the ledge, descend slightly to reach the foot of twin grooves, climb the right one 30 ft. to belay. Continue by the groove to the top of the buttress, 200 ft. *Diagram*, p. 184.

The following two routes are in effect girdle traverses of the buttress.

165 The High Girdle   1345 ft.   Severe

I. S. Clough and K. Sutcliffe,   1 June, 1961.

Climb the easy groove left of Mourning Slab, 200 ft. Belay on the left edge. Continue to a grass ledge on the edge above on the right; traverse up into the foot of the corner then down to the ledge and belays on Mourning Slab, 60 ft. Traverse up rightwards to the diagonal crack, climb this then descend to stance and chock belay. Move up a few feet then traverse to a grass ledge and belay, 60 ft. Cross the chimney of Route I and descend to the junction with Route II, 50 ft. Follow Route II to the outer edge of the buttress, 275 ft. Continue by a grassy traverse to Evening Wall and block belays, 90 ft. Follow a broad ledge, under a blank wall, passing large block belays, to join Orgy, 130 ft. Go round the corner then up leftwards by ledges to belay at a large block beneath a bulging corner, 70 ft. Climb the crack above and continue to a large scree covered terrace, 100 ft. Climb more easily for 200 ft. to the top. *Diagram*, p. 170.

166 **The Orgy** 2000 ft. Very Severe

I. S. Clough and K. Sutcliffe, 31 May, 1961.

Climb the minor buttress of Route I then from the start of the chimney traverse upwards to the right to gain a groove; descend 6 ft. then follow a gangway between the overlaps to belays (thread runner at the top of the gangway) 80 ft. Move right to a grassy groove, descend to a spike, 40 ft. Ascend once more then traverse on the same line rising slightly to reach another groove; descend a few feet then cross to a grass ledge and belays on Centurion, 50 ft. Descend Centurion to the corner and peg belay at the top of pitch 3, 160 ft. A horizontal traverse is made to the right above the overhangs and below the overlap. At 60 ft. climb up to the right, jammed knot runner (peg on first ascent), then descend a crack for 10 ft. and traverse to a stance and belay on the nose overlooking the corner of The Bat, 80 ft. Climb the slab rightwards across The Bat to the left edge of the great corner of Sassenach. Climb a bulge and continue near the edge to the 'grassy terrace' on Sassenach, 110 ft. Descend Sassenach to the foot of the chimney section, 170 ft., then traverse rightwards (the Patey Traverse) and descend to a stance on Titan's Wall, peg belay, 60 ft. Continue rightwards along the ledge until a peg enables a move into the crack in the corner on the right (Shield Direct); continue by the crack to a large block belay at the foot of The Shield, 110 ft. Climb directly for 20 ft. (peg) to a wide ledge then traverse into The Shield, 70 ft. Climb The Shield to its junction with Evening Wall, 300 ft. Move up to the left and follow a zigzag line of gangways and short walls to a grass ledge, 130 ft. Above on the left is a large block below a bulging corner, climb this 100 ft., continue in 200 ft. to the top. *Diagram*, p. 170.

167   **Waterfall Gully**   700 ft.   IV

D. Pipes, I. S. Clough, J. M. Alexander, R. Shaw and A. Flegg, 7 and 8 January, 1959.

The gully defines the North flank of the Great Buttress of Càrn Dearg, rising initially in one great step over 100 ft. high, thereafter easily to gain the saddle behind the pinnacle of the Staircase Climb.

On the first ascent, the party prepared the barrier pitch one day, then ascended the gully the next, taking seven hours overall. The gully has subsequently been ascended as a straightforward climb. Climb directly on ice by a shallow chimney, turn a bulge at 40 ft. (peg runner) then up and back left on iced slabs to a peg belay, 75 ft. Continue on easier angled ice to reach the upper gully in 40 ft. After one short ice pitch, snow leads without difficulty to the gully exit.

Slabby rocks in the exit area may present a hazard and parties should take care when avalanche conditions prevail. Allow 4–7 hours for the ascent. *Diagram*, p. 184.

168   **Staircase Climb**   Very Difficult

J. H. B. Bell, J. Maclay and W. W. Naismith,   12 July, 1898.

Start up to the right of the Evening Wall Route by the

higher of two shelves sloping up round a corner to the right.

Once round the corner, follow the stepped slab up rightwards to the foot of a clean cut crack in a corner, 50 ft. Climb the crack then a short wall above to a platform, belay, 25 ft. Continue by a chimney above to reach easy ground, 50 ft. Scramble by the crest of the buttress making for a conspicuous pinnacle, 200 ft. Turn the pinnacle on the left descending a few feet into Waterfall Gully, then up, to climb a steep slab giving access to the saddle beyond the pinnacle. Climb the left hand of the two chimneys above for 150 ft. to reach easier climbing following a ridge up leftwards to gain the summit rocks of the Great Buttress of Càrn Dearg. *Diagrams*, pp. 182, 184.

VARIATIONS

168a **Straight Chimney** 130 ft. Severe

B. P. Kellett, C. M. Plackett and R. L. Plackett, 22 June, 1944.

From the raking shelf at the start of the original route, some 50 ft. right of Waterfall Gully is a deep cut, smooth sided chimney. Climb the chimney, strenuous and awkward to a chockstone belay, 40 ft. Climb more easily to effect a junction with Raeburn's Variation which traverses into the upper section of this chimney, 90 ft. Finish as for that route.

168b 150 ft. Very Difficult

H. Raeburn and A. E. Robertson, 6 July, 1903.

From the platform above the 'clean cut crack and short wall' on the original route descend a broad shelf to the left to turn an exposed corner. Move up leftwards by large steps until a deep cut chimney is reached, 60 ft. Climb the chimney to reach the easier rocks leading to the pinnacle, 50 ft.

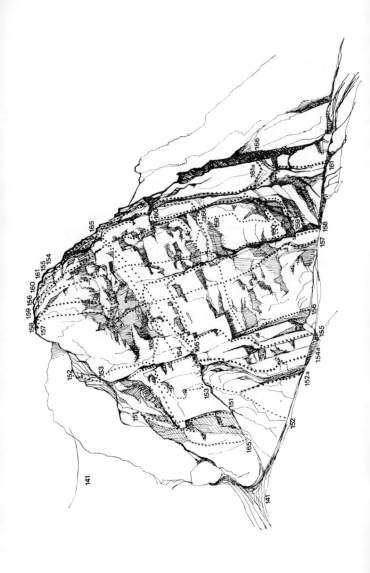

168c   **Deep Chimney**   130 ft.   Difficult

B. P. Kellett, C. M. Plackett and R. L. Plackett,   22 June, 1944.

From the neck behind the pinnacle climb the right hand of the twin chimneys.

WINTER   IV

D. Haston and J. Stenhouse,   February 1957.

Climb snow and ice glazed rock to the 'clean cut crack', this can be awkward if verglaced (on the first ascent under these conditions a peg was used). The pitch above presented mixed rock and ice climbing thereafter steep snow was ascended to the pinnacle. Ice was encountered on the section above the neck, followed by snow slopes leading to the summit. Allow 4 hours.

If there is a light cover of snow the turning of the pinnacle can prove a difficult problem.

North Wall of Càrn Dearg

This is the name given to the Northern flank of the Càrn Dearg Buttress. Although traversed by several large ledges, the intervening walls are impressively steep and provide fine climbs. Routes up this wall were made by Dr. Luscher in 1920 and by Nelstrop and Byrom in 1940—S.M.C.J. 23.1.46. Accounts of these ascents have proved impossible to reconcile with the actual buttress, although it is probable that both eventually ascended the wall by the final pitches of Route 'B'.

169 **Macphee's Route**   300 ft.   Very Difficult
G. G. Macphee and H. V. Hughes,   24 June, 1931.

From the lowest leftmost point of the North wall follow a grass shelf on the crest to a vegetated chimney. Climb this to a grass ledge, 60 ft. Continue by the chimney above with a hard exit at 70 ft. to reach the leftmost end of Easy Way and Broad Terrace. Climb the broken crack on the left, traverse left onto the slab rib at 20 ft. and continue by slabs to a belay on Flake Terrace, 60 ft. The crack can be climbed throughout but this eliminates the best situation on the climb.

The steep wall above is unclimbed and the route now traverses Flake Terrace, involving an awkward descent behind a large flake, to reach the Crevasse. From this point the higher routes can be followed to the top or the ledge continued to reach the foot of the face *via* the lower pitches of Harrison's Route. *Diagram*, p. 182.

170   **Zag-Zig**   180 ft.   Severe

I. S. Clough, R. Porteous, P. Brocklehurst and R. Henson,   28 May,
     1959.

This follows the obvious zigzag fault up the steep wall
below Easy Way. Climb up to the grassy lower crack then
traverse it to a stance and belay, 90 ft. Move right up the
chimney by a stomach traverse; half-way one is forced onto
the wall. The finish is an awkward exit from a cave well
protected by chockstone runners. *Diagram*, p. 182.

171   **Easy Way**   150 ft.   Easy
     This is a broad grass rake which starts about 150 ft.
along the wall from the left end of the face. *Diagram*, p. 182.

172   **Broad Terrace**   200 ft.   Easy
     This terrace traverses rightwards from the termination
of Easy Way across the face to join Flake Terrace. *Diagram*,
p. 182.

173   **Flake Chimney**   100 ft.   Moderate

B. P. Kellett,   10 August, 1943.

Start to the right of Easy Way at a large flake with a deep
chimney to the right. Climb the chimney to exit by a window
in the flake, 80 ft. Scramble to Broad Ledge, 20 ft. *Diagram*,
p. 182.

174   **Direct Start to Route B**   70 ft.
                                          Very Difficult

B. P. Kellett and C. M. Plackett,   1943.

From Broad Ledge, just above Flake Chimney climb to
the foot of conspicuous crack, 10 ft. belay. Climb the crack
which is strenuous in the lower reaches to gain the crest of
Flake Terrace, 60 ft. *Diagram*, p. 182.

175   **Route B**   100 ft.   Severe

B. P. Kellett, J. H. B. Bell and M. Forsyth,   11 August, 1943.

Start some 20 ft. right of the finish of the Direct Start, on the secondary point of the Flake Terrace and under a large recess in the upper wall.

From the flake gain a groove in the steep wall and climb to the grass recess, 25 ft. belays. Make an exposed traverse right onto a rib then climb directly by a crack to gain easier rocks, 40 ft., belay. Continue by the crack to Diagonal Terrace and a block belay, 25 ft. *Diagram*, p. 182.

176   **Route A**   300 ft.   Severe

B. P. Kellett,   2 July, 1943.

Traverse along Diagonal Terrace to the right for 50 ft. to an open corner. Climb to the right of the corner to a ledge and thread belay beneath a steep, exposed slab with two thin cracks, 20 ft., belay. Climb up then gain the cracks by a difficult move left, continue directly for 50 ft. then more easily up to the right to a right angled corner, 90 ft. There are escape routes to the right at the start and finish of this pitch. Quit the corner by bridging on small holds to reach Green Terrace, 20 ft. Easier climbing by slabs leads to the top of the buttress at a point some 60 ft. below the top of Waterfall Gully, 150 ft. Belays on this section are poor. *Diagram* p. 182.

177   **Caterpillar Crawl**   150 ft.   Severe

B. Ritchie, J. Mills, C. Pattinson and R. Hill,   24 June, 1949.

Climb the first three pitches of Route A. From the corner descend a few feet and make a traverse to the right along a narrow ledge until it is possible to stand; continue delicately to reach a spike belay, 50 ft. Move right until the short wall above can be climbed then follow an obvious line of holds up left to a stance behind a block, 25 ft. Climb the wall above to a mossy recess, belay high up, 25 ft. Descend a few feet, round the rib on the left then up until the grooves on the right can be entered and climbed to the top, 45 ft. *Diagram*, p. 182.

178   **Flake Terrace**   200 ft.   Difficult

From above the first pitch of Harrison's Route climb up to the left by a series of easy chimneys to gain the highest point of the ledge. This terrace can be used as an access to the upper routes of the buttress or as a descending extension of Macphee's Route. *Diagram*, p. 182.

179   **Harrison's Climb**   900 ft.   Difficult

A. Harrison, G. M. Lawson and W. N. Allan,   12 June, 1929.

The right-hand edge of the face is defined by deep chimney separating the North Wall of Càrn Dearg from Cousin's Buttress.

Start 40 ft. left of the chimney at a small platform of rock. Climb a 20 ft. pitch to easier ground which is followed up rightwards into a deep chimney. Climb the chimney then more easily by its continuation to gain the saddle behind the top of Cousin's Buttress. Traverse left below a smooth face, pass an awkward corner to gain a grass ledge leading to easy ground which is followed for 300 ft., to reach a wide corrie. The right edge of a water course in the centre of this corrie is then followed to the foot of a chimney leading through the final rocks. A through route leads past the first chockstone; the second is climbed on the right to gain a shallow gully. Higher up an overhanging pitch is turned by two huge flakes. The final chockstone pitch is turned on the right whence a short climb leads to the summit. *Diagram*, p. 182.

179a **Variation**   70 ft.   Very Difficult

A. Horn and H. V. Hughes, 25 June, 1931.

Start 40 ft. right of Harrison's Climb to ascend the deep chimney, 70 ft. This makes a direct line with the upper chimney, giving access to the saddle behind Cousin's Buttress.

WINTER   III

C. G. M. Slessor and N. Tennant, 1961.

The approaches into the chimney gully are normally banked up, but occasionally a large build up of ice can occur on this section. Within the gully, climb an ice pitch 40 ft., then snow to the saddle behind Cousin's Buttress.

Above the traverse to the upper section of the buttress the rocks are normally masked by a large ice fall; climb this near the right edge by steep ice, 100 ft. An easier angle then leads to the upper corrie where a selection of routes can be followed to the summit.

180 **Dungeon Variation**   300 ft.   Very Difficult

I. M. Brooker and A. D. Lyall, 2 July, 1949.

Climb the original route to the saddle. Move into a grassy chimney on the right and climb in two pitches to a cave beneath two chockstones. Continue by a through route to an exit 30 ft. above the second chockstone, belay. Traverse to a flake, climb up then make another traverse to enter the foot of a gully which is followed to easier climbing leading up to the summit rocks of Càrn Dearg. *Diagram*, p. 182.

Cousin's Buttress

The buttress appears as a sentinel flake or pinnacle some 200 ft. high, abutting the North Wall of Càrn Dearg. Separated by a deep chimney gully from the main wall, it presents a steep narrow face to the North-east and, to the North a less steep wall broken by two large grass ledges. These ledges run out rightwards to join the easy approach gully of Raeburn's Buttress which lies further to the right.

181 **Direct Route**   200 ft.   Severe

B. P. Kellett, 20 August, 1944.

This route ascends the North face of the buttress avoiding the gully altogether. Climb to the first of two big grass ledges on the North face, alternatively walk on from the gully. Start up to the second ledge from the right, after 30 ft. traverse left by a slab to gain a crack in the corner. Follow the crack to the left end of the second grass ledge, 70 ft. Climb the steep rocks on the left to below a small flake visible from the ledge. Climb a bulge onto the top of the flake, traverse left, surmount a short wall and scramble to the top of the buttress, 100 ft. *Diagram,* p. 182.

182 **Ordinary Route**   750 ft.   Very Difficult

C. W. Walker and H. Walker, 11 June, 1904.

Climb the gully to the right of the buttress on water-worn rocks, 60 ft. Traverse left onto the second grass ledge to climb directly by steep rock for 40 ft., then scramble to the top of the buttress, 100 ft. From the saddle gain the wall beyond and traverse left past an awkward corner to a grass ledge. A few feet along the ledge break up rightwards to climb a rock rib for 200 ft. to a large scree slope. Scrambling then leads to the steep rocks under the summit of Càrn Dearg; climb these slightly to the right of the actual summit. *Diagram*, p. 182.

WINTER   III

C. H. C. Brunton and J. Clarkson,   14 February, 1957.

Climb the approach gully with one short ice pitch until level with the top of Cousin's Buttress then traverse out on steep snow to the junction with the North Wall of Càrn Dearg. Normally this is masked by a large ice fall which is climbed by the right edge and can involve steep ice climbing of about 100 ft. Above this point easier angle snow ice leads in 80 ft. to the upper corrie whence a choice of routes lead to the summit.

Càrn Dearg Summit Buttress

Above the Staircase, Cousin's and Raeburn's buttresses is a small hanging corrie. The upper face leads almost to the summit of Càrn Dearg and contains the three gullies and buttresses recorded below. When first climbed, the party gained the corrie from the upper reaches of Ledge Route by an easy descent. (As for Girdle Traverse).

183 **Colando Gully**   600 ft.   II

I. S. Clough and D. Pipes, 12 April, 1958.

This is the winding gully on the left and is steep snow, with occasionally a short ice pitch. (This gully is actually the final section of Harrison's Route).

Allow 1½–2 hours for the ascent.

184 **Arch Buttress**   600 ft.   III

D. Pipes and A. Flegg, 3 January, 1959.

Start between the Colando and Arch Gullies.

Climb by the crest, 150 ft., then slightly rightward into a groove. At the top make an awkward move left to reach a platform then up 100 ft. to a snow patch. Move right, climb the chimney (crux) then make a long stride left up into the centre of three chimneys, 100 ft., then easily to the summit.

185 **Arch Gully**   600 ft.   I

I. S. Clough and D. Pipes, 12 April, 1958.

This separates the middle buttresses and gives a steep uncomplicated snow climb. Allow 1½–2 hours for the ascent.

186   **Surprise Buttress**   800 ft.   III

I. S. Clough and B. Halpin,   3 January, 1959.

Traverse onto the buttress from the foot of Arch Gully.

After a short groove traverse back to the left edge of the buttress which is followed as closely as possible for 300 ft. until above the Arch in the gully and below the final wall. Traverse right beneath the wall until above Surprise Gully, 100 ft. Climb short walls slightly left to a small ledge and block belay some 30 ft. above the traverse. Step down and right to climb a steep groove, strenuous, 120 ft. Finish by easier climbing to the Càrn Dearg Summit.

187   **Surprise Gully**   600 ft.   II

I. S. Clough and D. Pipes,   12 April, 1958.

The gully is shallow with a broken rock rib splitting the lower section. This is straightforward for 400 ft. then 100 ft. of scrambling leads to final rocks which are climbed by an icy groove. Allow $1\frac{1}{2}$–2 hours for the ascent.

188   **Baird's Buttress**   300 ft.   Very Difficult

P. D. Baird and E. J. A. Leslie,   18 June, 1938.

This buttress lies at the rightmost reaches of the upper corrie, i.e. just before the rocks adjoin the upper section of Raeburn's Buttress.

Start from the ledge of the Girdle Traverse which can be gained from Raeburn's Buttress or by descending the upper corrie from Ledge Route. The route follows the crack splitting the front of the buttress. Climb the crack in two steep sections, 80 ft. A steep wall above leads to easier climbing which continues to the top of the buttress. *Diagram*, p. 184.

Raeburn's Buttress

This is the slender tapering buttress between the main mass of Càrn Dearg and the Castle. From some viewpoints the buttress appears almost as a pinnacle.

189 **Raeburn's Route**   750 ft.   Very Difficult

H. Raeburn, H. MacRobert and D. S. Arthur,   28 September, 1908.

Start up the gully on the left (South) side of the buttress. Climb easy water-worn rocks for 200 ft. to a point where the gully bifurcates to form two chimneys. Climb the right branch to a cave and belay, 100 ft.; exit by the right wall and gain a chockstone. Traverse right into a chimney gully and belay, 80 ft. Follow the gully easily to a pitch giving access to the terrace on the neck of the buttress, 100 ft. Alternatively traverse right onto the crest of the buttress and climb to the terrace. (Girdle Traverse). Climb the crest of the buttress to finish by a vertical step and a narrow arête to reach the easier slopes of the mountain, 270 ft. *Diagrams*, pp. 182, 184.

WINTER   III

W. D. Brooker and J. M. Taylor,   31 January, 1959.

Steep snow with short ice pitches lead up to the cave pitch; this usually provides a 30 ft. ice pitch. Thereafter follow the grooves or arête depending upon prevailing conditions. Allow 3–5 hours for the ascent.

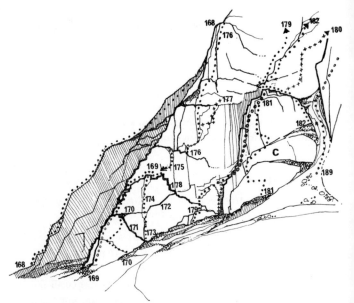

NORTH WALL OF CÀRN DEARG

189a **Variation**   200 ft.   III

G. G. Macphee, R. Ashley and C. H. Oates,   14 April, 1938.

From the cave on the original route, instead of climbing
the right wall continue up the gully to a cave exit at the top.

190 **Continuation Wall**   270 ft.   Severe

T. Weir, I. McNicol and A. McNicol,   7 October, 1951.

Climb the original route to where the introductory gully
bifurcates. Take the left branch and climb water-worn slabs
to a ledge on the left, poor belays, 60 ft. Climb the continuation of the chimney by back and foot; exit left to belay,
50 ft. Continue up the gully, now easy, to below a steepening,
100 ft. Climb up and left to gain a narrow crack. Climb this to
enter a chimney leading to a ledge (Girdle Traverse) 60 ft.

191 **The Crack**   600 ft.   Very Severe

H. A. Carsten and T. McGuinness,   16 June, 1946.

This is the conspicuous crack splitting the steep front
of the buttress.

Quit the lower rocks in the introductory gully of the
Original Route and scramble up rightwards making for
the foot of the crack. Access to the crack is barred by decep-
tively difficult, vegetated slabs. Climb these rightwards to
gain a ledge then traverse to block belays, 50 ft. A peg was
used on this pitch on the first ascent. Climb the crack,
surmounting an overhang, to reach a platform on the right,
50 ft., peg belay. Continue by the crack to a chockstone;
climb another overhang then more easily to a ledge and
belay on the left, 70 ft. Climb the crack over yet another
overhang then up to a ledge and belay on the left. Continue
by the crack to reach easier rocks and a junction with the
Original Route, 100 ft. Finish by the crest as for that route,
300 ft. *Diagram,* p. 184.

TITAN'S WALL – THE CASTLE RIDGE

CD   Càrn Dearg Buttress
SB   Càrn Dearg Summit Buttress
RB   Raeburn's Buttress
CB   Cousin's Buttress
C   The Castle
CR   Castle Ridge
nw   North Wall of Càrn Dearg

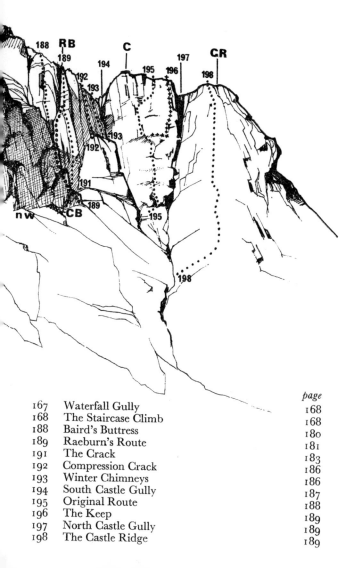

192   **Compression Crack**   400 ft.   Very Difficult

C. F. Rolland and H. I. Ogilvy,   21 June, 1940.

Scramble by easy slabs and grass ledges above the left
wall of South Castle Gully to reach a well defined ledge
(Girdle Traverse) beneath a chimney corner, half-way along
the steep Northern wall of the final section of Raeburn's
Buttress. This ledge can be gained by traversing right from
the foot of the final arête of Raeburn's Buttress. This is a
section of the Girdle Traverse. Climb on clean, water-worn
rocks following the chimney in two pitches of 40 ft. and 80ft.,
strenuous and becoming progressively more difficult.
Above the chimney, break up to the left over slabs to the
top of Raeburn's Buttress, 120 ft. *Diagram,* p. 184.

193   **Winter Chimneys**   425 ft.   Severe

I. S. Clough and G. Grandison,   11 June, 1962.

Follow the terrace beyond Compression Crack for 100 ft.
to the foot of a deep chimney, topped by huge capstone.

Climb the chimney, 20 ft., belay. Continue up to the
capstone, with difficulty move to the outside, then up to
stance and belays, 40 ft. Continue in the same line past a
steep corner to easy ground, 70 ft. Move rightwards to belay
at the foot of a wide chimney, 100 ft. Climb outside a deep
narrow chimney, within the depths of the main chimney,
to make an awkward exit, to a stance and chockstone belay,
40 ft. A through route leads under the big chockstone to
easier climbing, 150 ft. *Diagram,* p. 184.

WINTER   IV

I. S. Clough and R. Sefton,   29 January, 1960.

From the belay above the first pitch a right traverse was
made to ascend a bulging crack on pegs to gain the stance
above the great capstone, 60 ft. The line above was followed

70 ft. then a leftward traverse made to enter the fan shaped corrie leading out to the summit slopes on Càrn Dearg.

194 **South Castle Gully**   700 ft.   Very Difficult

*H. MacRobert, R. E. Workman, Mrs. and Miss Inglis Clark,
    15 July, 1911.*

The gully divides the Castle from Raeburn's Buttress.

Scramble to the first chockstone pitch. Climb this by a crack on the left, 25 ft. The second chockstone pitch is climbed on the right to under the chockstone, thread belay, 25 ft. Continue up to the right and into the gully bed. The pitch above is climbed by the right wall to reach some large boulders, 50 ft. Scramble for 300 ft., surmount a short chockstone pitch then continue without difficulty for 200 ft. to a pitch of reddish rock. Climb by a crack on the left; continue by the gully over short easy pitches to the plateau. *Diagram*, p. 184.

194a **Variation**   Very Difficult

G. G. Macphee and A. G. Murray,   29 September, 1935.

Climb the third pitch by a slanting ledge on the left wall.

WINTER   I

*W. Brunskill, W. W. King and W. W. Naismith,   1 April,
    1896.*

Under normal conditions the gully provides an uncomplicated snow ascent.

Parties should take care when bad conditions prevail as the rock formation of the gully make it prone to avalanche. Allow 2–3 hours for the ascent.

The Castle

195 **Original Route**   700 ft.   Very Difficult

H. Raeburn and T. Gibson, 11 September, 1898.

Start beneath the undercut nose of the buttress at a slabby break. Climb overhanging rock on good holds for 12 ft. then more easily to belay, 25 ft. Continue by scrambling, bearing slightly left to reach a shallow gully which gives access to a grass terrace under the upper slabs, 400 ft. Climb the slabs slightly right then left by an awkward corner and move left into a chimney, 70 ft. Follow the chimney to a chockstone belay, 60 ft. Break out by the right wall, past an awkward corner then by slabs to a shallow gully which leads to a grass bay and belay, 70 ft. Climb slabs on the right then a short chimney, 40 ft., belay. More slabs on the right lead to a short wall which gives access to the top of the buttress. *Diagram*, p. 184.

WINTER   III

W. Brown, J. Maclay, W. W. Naismith and G. Thomson,
     April 1896.

A cone of avalanche snow often masks the first pitch to render it easy. Steep snow is then followed up the centre of the buttress. Near the top if the slabs are iced the climb will provide considerable difficulties.

The slab character of the buttress creates a tendency to avalanche and the ascent should not be attempted when such conditions prevail. Allow 3–4 hours for the ascent.

196   **The Keep**   250 ft.   Severe

J. M. Alexander and I. S. Clough,   29 June, 1958.

Climb the original route for some 400 ft. to exit from the
shallow gully. A grass terrace leads under the upper slabs
to the right; traverse down to a corner and block belay.
Climb above the belay to a ledge, move right and follow a
groove to a grass ledge, 50 ft., block belay. Climb onto a
projecting block and continue to a good stance and belay,
40 ft. Climb a groove, surmount a bulge then continue to
reach easier climbing and a flake belay, 60 ft. The groove
continues but a better finish is by the slab edge on the left,
100 ft. *Diagram,* p. 184.

197   **North Castle Gully**   700 ft.   Difficult

F. Greig, A. E. McKenzie and A. N. Other,   19 September,
     1904.

This gully separates the Castle from the Castle Ridge.

Climb scree till about midheight where a double chockstone pitch is turned by the right wall, 40 ft. Higher up two
short chockstone pitches are climbed. About 100 ft. from
the top a mossy chimney is avoided by crossing slabs to
climb a chimney on the right then easily to the plateau.
Diagram, p. 184.

WINTER   I

J. H. B. Bell and R. G. Napier,   4 April, 1896.

The gully gives an uncomplicated snow ascent; there is
rarely a large cornice. Allow 2–3 hours for the ascent.

198   **Castle Ridge**   900 ft.   Moderate

J. N. Collie, W. W. Naismith, G. Thomson and M. W. Travers,
     12 April, 1895.

The ridge is mainly scrambling with a few moderate
pitches but its ascent presents fine views.

Start at the lowest point of the buttress. The lower rocks are crossed by ledges raking up rightwards which tend to lead the climber onto the right wall of the buttress. Maintain the direct line by crossing a succession of slabs to gain some huge detached blocks, 300 ft. Continue by the steeper rocks above to an almost level section of the ridge, 250 ft. (This point can be gained more easily from the foot of North Castle Gully). The steep rocks above are climbed by a 30 ft. chimney then more easily to another steep section climbed by a 40 ft. chimney. The ridge now narrows. A steep rib can be climbed by thin cracks but several routes are possible. The angle then relents and scrambling leads to the top of the ridge.

An easy descent can be made down the slopes on the right or North over an extensive boulder field to the Lochan Meall An t-Suidhe. *Diagram*, p. 184.

WINTER   III

The ridge is best gained from below the Castle Gullies. In good conditions it provides a fine winter climb which should always be possible to a competent party. Difficulties are generally turned on the left. Allow 3–5 hours for the ascent.

North Wall of Castle Ridge

The following routes are located on the great Northern wall of the Castle Ridge. The wall is considerably broken up with only winter routes recorded to date.

199 **The Serpent**   1000 ft.   II

I. S. Clough, D. Pipes and J. Porter, 12 February, 1959.

A steep snow climb. Start near the left edge of the face at a small gully above the Luncheon Stone. Climb the gully then by a shelf curving rightwards reach the lower section of another gully, 500 ft. Follow this to the shoulder of Càrn Dearg. Allow $1\frac{1}{2}$–$2\frac{1}{2}$ hours for the ascent.

200 **Nordwand**   1400 ft.   III

I. S. Clough, D. Pipes, B. Sarll, F. Jones and J. Porter,
   11 February, 1959.

Start in a small gully near the right edge of the face; after 80 ft. break out left onto the buttress or, alternatively, continue by an ice pitch in the gully. Traverse left to gain a natural line of ascent which is followed until 700 ft. up the face. At this point a gully comes in from the left (The Serpent). Cross this and climb steep snow for 400 ft. to the foot of the summit rocks. These are ascended by a series of walls and traverses leading to the left to gain the final rocks of the Castle Ridge. Time taken on this ascent 5 hours.

201 **La Petite**   600 ft.   III

I. S. Clough, D. Pipes and J. Porter, 12 February, 1959.

This follows the obvious gully near the right edge of the North Wall.

Start 100 ft. right of Nordwand, climb ice for 80 ft. to peg belay then 40 ft. up steep rock. Finish by the gully which has further ice pitches of 60 ft. each. Allow 3–4 hours for the ascent.

202   **Girdle Traverse**   Severe

J. H. B. Bell, and J. D. B. Wilson,   21 September, 1941.

This is a fine expedition over relatively easy ground other than the section approaching Point Five Gully.

Start from Càrn Mor Dearg Arête, cross to the 'second platform' of the North East Buttress, make for the V-notch and traverse to the 'basin', continue to cross Zero Gully to Observatory Ridge. A curving ledge leads on to cross Point Five Gully above the top of Rubicon Wall. Walk across to the foot of the Great Tower, cross Glover's Chimney, traverse to Number Two Gully and ascend Comb Gully, to Hesperides Ledge and Green Gully and so on to Number Three Gully. Cross Creag Coire na Ciste to Number Four Gully then by some slopes cross the Trident Buttress and Càrn Dearg Buttress face, to South Castle Gully, the Castle and North Castle Gully to Castle Ridge.

WINTER   IV

J. R. Marshall and T. W. Patey,   31 January, 1959.

This is a winter traverse from right to left of the section extending from Observatory Gully to the Càrn Mor Dearg Arête.

From the foot of Gardyloo Gully traverse snow bands leftwards by a descending line to enter Point Five Gully. Ascend a short distance, then cross iced slabs (a tension traverse was made on the first crossing) to easier ground leading to Observatory Ridge. Cross Zero Gully, descend to the 'basin' then follow the obvious raking snow ramp of the V-Traverse to gain the crest of North East Buttress. An ascending traverse now leads round the buttress to the final slopes of Càrn Mor Dearg Arête. Allow 5–8 hours for the expedition.

202a   Red Gully   400 ft.   II

D. *Pipes, I. S. Clough, J. Porter, B. Sarll and H. Fisher,*
    11 February, 1959.

This gully splits the small buttress which lies to the right of the North Wall of Castle Ridge.

A straightforward snow gully presenting one short ice pitch. Allow 1½–2 hours for the ascent.

Glen Nevis Gullies

South-west of the col between Ben Nevis and Càrn Dearg, S.W., 3348 ft., is a slope gradually steepening down into Glen Nevis. Near the top there are some crags, but climbs on these are not very continuous. Although many scrambles have been made, no definite rock-climbs are recorded. This place can be reached by traversing along the mountainside in continuation of the pony track after it has crossed the Red Burn, before turning up towards the summit of Ben Nevis. Further along this slope are the Glen Nevis Gullies. The foot of these can most easily be reached from the Glen Nevis Road.

203 **Achintee Gully**   400 ft.   Difficult
D. G. Duff,   2 September, 1947.

Achintee Gully is on the steep slope of Meall an t' Suidhe just above Achintee Farm. It has a number of moderate pitches and one of difficult standard. In icy conditions, good experience can be gained.

There is a right-hand branch continuing at the top which gives a further 200 ft. of climbing.

204 **Five Finger Gully**   500 ft.   Difficult

Five Finger Gully is the first major gully South of the Red Burn. It is a cascading river course with a few waterfalls and some interesting pitches.

205 **Antler Gully**   400 ft.   Difficult
D. G. Duff, J. Ness and R. Murphie,   30 May, 1947.

This gully is formed in the side of Càrn Dearg by erosion

of a friable granitic vein. It starts about 200 ft. North of the old graveyard.

There are about four 20 ft. pitches with problems of slab climbing mostly on the right or left walls and two pitches of 50 ft. What little water there is in it is usually avoidable.

206 **Surgeon's Gully** Without doubt, one of our major gullies. It is difficult to account for the neglect to which the climb is apparently subjected. Surprisingly, the gully still awaits a complete ascent, i.e. an ascent of the introductory, middle and upper central branch of the gully which would possibly result in the longest and most difficult gully climb in the country.

1500 ft.   Very Severe

D. H. Hawarth and G. Ritchie,   15 August, 1947.

Start to the right of Antler Gully and the old graveyard. Climb by small slabby pitches to the base of a major chockstone pitch. Climb to the cave, 60 ft., then exit by a slab on the right (this is the most difficult pitch in the gully to date and is very severe). Above this is the point at which the original ascent started with details as follows.

Pitch 1. A 25 ft. chockstoned pitch with an awkward start then back and foot until the top of the chockstone is reached. Exit on the left.

Pitch 2. 60 ft. Climb direct for 30 ft. then back and foot to turn the exit chockstone by the right wall.

Pitch 3. The gully is now followed with ease to the 'impasse' pitch, a magnificent section over 100 ft. high with a large chockstone in its upper reaches. Regrettably this is unclimbed and the route goes by the right wall about 30 ft. from the back of the gully.

Climb onto the wall for 15 ft., move left onto a rib, surmount an awkward ledge by a mantleshelf move, then another to gain a nose at the top of a slab on the left. Continue more easily to climb an awkward, 20 ft. open chimney, then delicately, scramble to finish.

Pitch 4. Traverse left round a rock corner and then continue for 50 ft.

Pitch 5. From a prominent block belay descend through trees to gain the gully bed some 30 ft. beyond the top of the impasse section, 50 ft.

Pitch 6. 40 ft. up a sloping rake on the left on very good holds.

Pitch 7. 15 ft. Chockstone pitch.

Pitch 8. 35 ft. Waterfall pitch. Start up left side and then traverse right into the waterfall and climb it direct.

Pitch 9. 20 ft. Chockstone, back and foot pitch.

Pitch 10. 20 ft. Waterfall pitch.

Pitch 11. 25 ft. Waterfall pitch.

Pitch 12. 25 ft. Easier angled sloping pitch.

Pitch 13. This is the last and most difficult pitch of the ascent. A large chockstone and attendant waterfall blocks the exit. Start a few feet back on the right wall; climb a smooth groove (delicate). Move right to a stance and running belay then continue 10 ft. to a stance and peg belay. Climb up 10 ft., surmount the nose on the left then traverse left into the waterfall to climb into a cave beneath the exit chockstone. From a good runner surmount the chockstone and climb to thread belay 25 ft. higher.

Pitch 14. 35 ft. Climb the rake along on the left side.

Pitch 15. 35 ft. Chockstone pitch turned on the left side with difficulty.

Pitches 14 and 15 can be avoided by an easy rake on the left wall.

Pitch 16. 15 ft. In a channel groove in the centre.

Pitch 17. 15 ft. Up the extreme right smooth groove.

Pitch 18. 60 ft. Waterfall pitch. Start on the right and

1. The waterfall is climbed half-way then traverse right

work obliquely left into it then straight up the bed of the waterfall from the halfway point.

Pitch 19. 120 ft. Climb the bed or water course to a large chockstone exit.

Pitch 20. 45 ft. Climb to the chockstone to turn it on the left.

Pitch 21. 30 ft. Continue by the bed to the final pitch which possesses the largest chockstone in the whole gully. Climb this either on the right or the left side.

This brings one to the horizontal deer track and fence and is the termination point of the original ascent. Above, the gully opens out to form three branches, the left section is a simple scramble, the central branch, very steep and apparently difficult and the right, patently more possible but still awaiting an ascent.

207 Christmas Gully   750 ft.   Very Difficult
J. G. Parish, H. Bell and H. Nicoll,   16 December, 1946.

This is the right hand gully on the South Face of Càrn Dearg, i.e. the first gully on the right below Polldubh. It is recognised by a prominent waterfall lower down. It is in three sections:

1. The waterfall is climbed half-way then traverse right and up to re-enter the gully higher up.

2. The gully opens out; several grassy pitches lead to a narrowing of the gully and a groove ascended by bridging then a steep wall avoided by a vegetatious pitch and another pitch above.

3. The 'Gorge'. About 500 ft. of short difficult pitches. Leave the gully and ascend the left wall then regain the gully to finish above a fork.

Polldubh Crags

Further along the glen where the road bridges the river at the lower Falls of Nevis, the Polldubh Crags can be seen located near the foot of the steep Southern slopes of the mountain.

With a frontage of nearly half a mile, they face South, provide a great variety of climbs on excellent rock and are often in good condition when the upper cliffs are not.

The buttresses are described from left to right as one proceeds up the glen.

Earlier exploration by members of Lochaber J.M.C.S., C.U.M.C., R.A.F. Mountain Rescue Units and C.D.M.C., must account for a considerable number of unrecorded ascents on these crags.

SHEEP FLANK BUTTRESS
This is located almost opposite the bridge and a little above the scree. *Diagram*, p. 212.

208   **Sheep Flank Wall**   200 ft.   Difficult
Start to the right of the overhanging base. Climb by a slab and crack; then follow the crest.

HANGOVER BUTTRESS
This stands above some large boulders about 200 yds. from the bridge. A large overhang is a prominent characteristic of the buttress. *Diagram*, p. 212.

209   **Route I**   200 ft.   Very Difficult

Start at the lowest rocks to climb a rib and continue to a grass ledge. Climb a short wall; traverse right by an awkward corner to finish above the overhang.

210   **Route II**   Severe

I. S. Clough, R. C. Mason, P. Hannon and O. S. Cook,   31 August, 1957.

Start left of, and climb directly to the overhang; traverse beneath it for 20 ft. then finish by a groove above.

211   **Route III**   Very Severe

I. S. Clough, R. C. Mason, P. Hannon and O. S. Cook, 1 September, 1957.

Further to the right and slightly higher is a large overhang; climb this direct with pegs.

CAVALRY CRACK BUTTRESS

This is located about 200 yards beyond and a little lower than Hangover Buttress. It carries a few pines. *Diagram*, p. 212.

212   **Cavalry Crack**   60 ft.   Moderate

This lies to the left of the steep section of the buttress.

213   **Storm**   300 ft.   Very Severe

I. S. Clough and T. Sullivan,   3 May, 1959.

Start under the steep left edge of the buttress.

Climb the steep left-hand groove 20 ft. then gain the right-hand groove to climb to a ledge, 100 ft. Climb a crack 25 ft., then awkwardly rightwards to traverse left up to a prominent pine, 100 ft. (Alternatively climb all the crack).

Climb a groove, right of the pine, finish by a steep wall above to a peg belay on the buttress edge, 50 ft. (This was originally climbed by using pegs but now often climbed free). Finish by a groove on the left 50 ft.

It is possible to make an escape route from the pine belay by a stomach traverse to the right (severe).

214   **Heat Wave**   370 ft.   Very Difficult

I. S. Clough, Miss J. Pickering, C. Anderson, R. Henson, P. Brocklehurst and R. Porteous,   2 May, 1959.

Start at the left-hand edge of the buttress.

Climb the groove (with holly at foot) for 20 ft.; step left into other groove then, reaching a tree, climb up to a heather ledge below the diagonal crack of Storm (belays). Traverse right round the corner to a ledge and tree belay below a vegetatious gully. Follow the gully a few feet then climb by a wall and slabs on the left to a ledge and belays. Finish up slabs.

215   **Vampire**   320 ft.   Very Severe

I. S. Clough and E. Buckley,   21 April, 1959.

Start 30 ft. right of the left edge of the buttress (cairn and arrow).

Climb the wall to a ledge and tree belay, 25 ft. Follow a rib on the left into a groove. Trend leftwards to gain a pine, belay, 75 ft. Walk to the foot of a groove, 25 ft. Climb the groove, then a wall; bear left on good holds to finish at the escape route for Storm, 100 ft. Climb slabs to finish, 120 ft.

216   **Fang**   140 ft.   Severe

W. Skidmore, P. McKenzie and J. Crawford,   July 1963.

This is a peg climb on the front of the buttress starting a few feet right of Vampire at a small overhang beneath a

tall steep wall (arrow). Climb the wall by an open groove
(pegs) to a big hold, 55 ft. Traverse left by an oblique
crack and gain a small ledge beneath another groove, peg
belay. Climb the groove (2 pegs) and surmount an overhang
on its right to reach an upper groove which is followed to a
large grass ledge at the top, 70 ft.

217 **G. String** 100 ft. Severe

R. R. Gray and G. Low, 2 May, 1965.

Start 10 ft. from the left edge of the violin shaped buttress
beside Storm.

Traverse left then up to the corner and continue obviously
to a niche at 80 ft. Surmount a short crack, 2 pegs and
continue to top.

SECRETARY'S CRACK BUTTRESS

This is located almost centrally among the crags and above
Cavalry Crack Buttress. It is easily identified by the rect-
angular form and the oblique crack raking up to the right,
across the face. *Diagram*, p. 212.

218 **Secretary's Crack** 250 ft. Very Difficult
Climb the chimney crack. From the top traverse left to
follow the slab crest of the buttress.

219 **Direct Route** 280 ft. Severe

I. S. Clough and E. Buckley, 21 April, 1959.

Climb the front of the buttress by a smooth slab corner
then by the thin central crack to gain the top of Secretary's
Crack. Finish by the slabs of that route.

220 **Last Word**   70 ft.   Very Severe

I. S. Clough,   22 May, 1959.

A hard alternative to the first pitch of the previous route.
Below Secretary's Crack is a parallel crack. Last Word
takes the steep wall below this.

PINNACLE RIDGE

This is located some 600 yards from the bridge and about
100 ft. above the road. Its slab face, is defined on the left
by a steep wall and to the right by overhanging rock.
Diagram, p. 212.

221 **Original Route**   150 ft.   Very Difficult

Climb from the lowest rocks to a small tree above the
vertical crack in the left wall.

Continue by a slab basin; traverse right by a large flake
then ascend the final slabs direct.

VARIATIONS

20 ft. Climb the vertical crack to the left wall, strenuous.
Severe.

20 ft. Climb the slabs to the right of the introductory
pitch. Severe.

222 **Mechanics Institute**   140 ft.   Severe

I. S. Clough, A. R. Lakin and A. Parkin,   5 April, 1959.

Start right of the severe slab variation. Climb an overhanging corner using pegs; regain rocks to finish on good
holds to a tree belay. Finish by a leftward spiral of the
buttress.

223 **Burma Road**   160 ft.   Severe

I. S. Clough and E. Buckley,   20 April, 1959.

Start between the severe slab variation and Mechanics Institute.

Climb the slab to a corner, reach holly to fight through the subsequent jungle to an overhang. Climb the right wall to a stance and tree belay. Traverse right by a heather ledge to belay (arrow). Climb slabs direct.

REPTON BUTTRESS

This is the first buttress above the Pinnacle Ridge. It has a conspicuous line of rounded overhangs. *Diagram*, p. 212.

224 **Repton**   150 ft.   Severe

T. Sullivan, E. Buckley and A. Flegg,   27 March, 1959.

Climb the middle of the face to a stance and tree belay below overhangs; traverse left for 30 ft. then, by a corner to a stance and tree belay. Continue by a small corner behind; break out right and up to finish.

PANDORA'S BUTTRESS

This is the second buttress above the Pinnacle Ridge. *Diagram*, p. 212.

225 **Phantom Slab**   190 ft.   Very Severe

T. Sullivan and I. S. Clough,   3 May, 1959.

Start at the foot of a rib left of, and 100 ft. above the start Pandora.

Climb the rib edge, 60 ft. Traverse to the foot of Dental Groove which is followed to the tree belay, 60 ft. Climb the steep slab on the left, 70 ft.

226 **Dental Groove**   110 ft.   Severe

I. S. Clough and E. Buckley,   20 April, 1959.

The obvious heathery groove half-way up the left-hand face of the buttress.

Difficult up to a tree belay; continue up the groove to join Pandora then up the wall to tree belays; climb slab on left.

227 **Pandora**   230 ft.   Severe

I. S. Clough and E. Buckley,   20 April, 1959.

Start on the left of the buttress.

Climb 100 ft. by clean slabs on the left to a large stance (belay high on the right). Climb the corner above for 10 ft., traverse to the left edge and follow the rib; round a corner, traverse below trees to another corner then climb the wall above to tree belays. Finally finish by a delicate slab on the left.

228 **Flying Dutchman**   220 ft.   Severe

T. Sullivan and I. S. Clough,   3 May, 1959.

Start at a rock tongue below and to the right of Pandora.

Go up the ridge crest to a grass terrace (tree belay); then climb slabs on the left, passing a small skyline tree.

229 **Degradation**   230 ft.   Severe

I. S. Clough and T. Sullivan,   3 May, 1959.

Follow slabs to the right of Flying Dutchman.

LITTLE BUTTRESS

This is situated above and to the right of Pandora's Buttress.
Diagram, p. 212.

230 **Spike**   160 ft.   Very Difficult

I. S. Clough, P. Brocklehurst, R. Henson and R. Porteous,   29 May,
    1959.

Climb clean slabs on front of the buttress to a tree.
Continue up, then traverse to buttress edge, stance and belay
above. Finish direct by the slab above (arrow).

231 **Tutor's Rib**   160 ft.   Very Difficult

I. S. Clough,   29 May, 1959.

Climb a few feet of Spike, traverse right to climb a rib.
Ascend the final slab some 10 ft. right of Spike.

PINE WALL BUTTRESS

This is located about 200 ft. above the Pinnacle Buttress and
some 200 yds. to the right. Probably best approached by
following the burn left of Pinnacle Ridge to its source where
the buttress can be identified by a pine tree at the top of the
second tier. *Diagram*, p. 212.

232 **Pine Wall**   300 ft.   Very Difficult

Start up from the left by a slab to a ledge under a steep,
reddish wall on the right. Climb this out onto an overhanging
corner then by easier rock to the pine. Climb the slab
above by a groove.

STYX BUTTRESS

This is located immediately right of Pine Wall Buttress.
It is steep with several overhangs. *Diagram*, p. 212.

233 **Doomsday**   100 ft.   Very Severe

I. S. Clough and J. M. Alexander,   28 June, 1958.

Start below the left wall of the buttress under a 20 ft.
diagonal chimney leading up to the left.

Climb the chimney then up right to a stance and poor belay, 35 ft. Climb the wall on the right using a peg and sling then finish by a dirty slab and groove, with the last few feet particularly difficult, 65 ft.

234   **Resurrection**   140 ft.   Very Severe
I. S. Clough and A. R. Lakin,   5 April, 1959.

Follow the long tapering slab up the left-hand side of the buttress (cairn); the difficulty is sustained.

235   **Tyke's Climb**   160 ft.   Very Difficult
E. Buckley and I. S. Clough,   20 April, 1959.

Start at left-hand edge of the buttress. Go up the middle of a 30 ft. slab then up a shattered ridge to a ledge, belay. Climb above, past a dead tree and up the ridge.

236   **Damnation**   95 ft.   Very Severe
I. S. Clough and J. M. Alexander,   28 June, 1958.

The route ascends the centre of the buttress.

Climb on to a large semi-detached flake and move round right on to a slab, 25 ft. Climb a wall on the right to a peg runner, reach the overhanging nose by a strenuous pull-up then trend left to a small stance and peg belay, 35 ft. Move right onto a slab and climb to finish, peg runner, 40 ft.

237   **Iche**   120 ft.   Very Severe
T. Sullivan and I. S. Clough,   11 April, 1959.

Start to the right of the diagonal heather groove splitting the front of the buttress.

Go up the slab to a poor stance (belay at right end of the overhang); traverse left, up a thin crack to a tree runner, then up leftward to finish.

238 **Fidelity**   140 ft.   Very Severe

Start 15 ft. right of a diagonal heather groove splitting the front of the buttress (cairn).

Go up the edge of the slab to a tree belay; continue directly up the rib on the left of a heather niche (belay); finish up the middle of the slab.

HIGH CRAG

This is the large two-tier buttress high up to the right of Secretary's Crack Buttress, above and left of Pine Wall. *Diagram*, p. 212.

239 **Hawk's Nest**   195 ft.   Severe

I. S. Clough and E. Buckley,   21 April, 1959.

On the second tier, starting 40 ft. above The Paunch. Climb up to a ledge with large blocks, thread belay, 15 ft. From an upper ledge descend a slab then, using a wedge, peg and sling, turn a corner. Swing into a groove under a roof and descend until above the Hawk's Nest. Climb a gangway on the right; turn a corner then traverse to a tree belay, 60 ft. Continue by a gully above to a chockstone belay, 60 ft. Climb the cracked wall on the left to a ledge on the buttress edge then finish by slabs, 60 ft.

240 **The Paunch**   240 ft.   Very Severe

I. S. Clough,   5 April, 1959.

On the second tier; start round the corner left of the gangway on Crag Lough Grooves, at the foot of a wall of red rock; overhanging for the first 15 ft. (cairn).

Climb the overhang to a stance and belay at 60 ft.; then 20 ft. to a tree belay. Another 40 ft. of scrambling

leads to a junction with Crag Lough Grooves. The final
120 ft. follows the slabs.

241   **Crag Lough Grooves**   500 ft.   Very Severe
I. Sullivan and I. S. Clough,   29 March, 1959.

The route ascends the left front of the buttress. Start to
the left of a cave overhang at the foot.

Climb a small corner to belay beneath overhangs, 40 ft.
Traverse rightward over ribs, 10 ft., to enter a groove then
climb this to heather ledge, 75 ft. Follow slabs above to a
large terrace which separates the buttress tiers, 130 ft.
Climb to and traverse an obvious gangway rightward to
turn a corner to reach a small stance and peg belay, 60 ft.
Climb the shallow groove and slabs above to a grass ledge,
70 ft. Finish by slabs, 120 ft.

242   **Kinloss Grooves**   240 ft.   Very Severe
I. S. Clough and T. Sullivan,   11 April, 1959.

Start at the first obvious break in the overhang right of
Crag Lough Grooves.

Climb the groove to a small stance beneath an overhang,
peg belay in place, 50 ft. Exit on the right and climb to a
recess; then by a groove and slabs above (tree belay), 90 ft.
Continue by slabs to a grass terrace at the top of the first tier,
100 ft.

243   **Hot Tin Roof**   220 ft.   Very Severe
T. Sullivan and I. S. Clough,   2 May, 1959.

Start 6 ft. right of Kinloss Grooves; the third break.
Climb the fault to a heather ledge, traverse left 10 ft., then
up to a pine tree. Continue diagonally rightward past
another tree to a small stance and peg belay, 100 ft. Climb
slabs, trending left, avoiding a heather groove, 120 ft.

244 **Enigma** 270 ft. Severe

T. Sullivan and I. S. Clough, 11 April, 1959.

Start at the right of the middle terrace left of a big recess.

Climb the slab to a heather groove at 30 ft. Traverse up left for 30 ft. to avoid a bulge, then 30 ft. back right and continue to a ledge and tree belay. Finish by slabs, 120 ft.

SCIMITAR BUTTRESS

This is the middle of three buttresses some 300 yards to the right of Pinnacle Ridge. It is about 300 yards above the road and has a sharp 15 ft. pinnacle at its base. *Diagram,* p. 212.

245 **Nutcracker Chimney** 50 ft. Severe

R. Wilkinson and D. Pipes, 8 April, 1958.

This lies on the left of the buttress.

246 **Diagonal Crack** 60 ft.

R. Wilkinson and D. Pipes, 8 April, 1958.

The crack lies to the right of the chimney. Climb the crack using seven pegs.

247 **Wanderlust** 120 ft. Very Difficult

I. S. Clough, 22 April, 1959.

Start right of Diagonal Crack.

Follow a fault, then traverse up left across the crack to finish by a rib.

MEALL CUMHANN

This crag is situated on the Southern slopes of the mountain, a little above the level floor of the glen, beyond the exit from the Glen Nevis Gorge. It is well seen from Steall Hut which stands just across the river.

The following routes were first ascended by the under-noted members of the R.A.F. Leconfield M.C.

F. K. Morallee, D. P. Lawson, H. R. Gartside, B. Collinson, B. Bellamy, R. Wallace and J. Freeman.

The climbs are described from left to right.

248 **Galax**   250 ft.   Very Difficult

1 March, 1953.

Climb a slab to an overhang, belay. Move out right then up slabs and blocks to belay. Traverse into a chimney, belay. Continue up and left to finish. *Diagram*, p. 212.

249 **Toadal**   250 ft.   Very Difficult

1 March, 1953.

Start under an ash tree, some 20 ft. up the broken heathery rocks. Climb to a shelf, then traverse left to a slab in the gully. Climb the slab, then to right under the overhang. Turn a corner, then by a wall to a tree belay beneath a shelf. Finish by a steep, strenuous chimney at the right end of the shelf. *Diagram*, p. 212.

250 **Flapjack Gully**   200 ft.   Difficult

1 March, 1953.

Climb the obvious gully with the large chockstone at mid-height. *Diagram*, p. 212.

251 **Route II**   200 ft.   Difficult

1 March, 1953.

Follow the narrow rib up the middle of the face. *Diagram*, p. 212.

252   **Route I**   150 ft.   Moderate

1 March, 1953.

Climb the right-hand ridge of the crag. *Diagram*, p. 212.

GRADED LIST OF ROCK CLIMBS

SEVERE

SEVERE

VERY DIFFICULT

VERY DIFFICULT

VERY DIFFICULT *continued*

DIFFICULT

DIFFICULT

MODERATE

EASY

GLEN NEVIS GULLIES

POLDUBH CRAGS